TECHNOLOGY, EDUCATION—CONNECTIONS
THE TEC SERIES

Series Editor: Marcia C. Linn
Advisory Board: Robert Bjork, Chris Dede, Joseph Krajcik, Carol Lee,
Jim Minstrell, Jonathan Osborne, Mitch Resnick, Constance Steinkuehler

How the Arts Can Save Education

Transforming Teaching, Learning, and Instruction

Erica Rosenfeld Halverson

Foreword by Ellen Weinstein,
in honor of Jacques d'Amboise

TEACHERS COLLEGE PRESS

TEACHERS COLLEGE | COLUMBIA UNIVERSITY
NEW YORK AND LONDON

Published by Teachers College Press,® 1234 Amsterdam Avenue, New York, NY 10027

Copyright © 2021 by Teachers College, Columbia University

Cover art and design, and all interior illustrations, by Lyra Evans.

Library of Congress Cataloging-in-Publication Data

Names: Halverson, Erica, author.
Title: How the arts can save education : transforming teaching, learning, and instruction / Erica Rosenfeld Halverson ; foreword by Ellen Weinstein.
Description: New York, NY : Teachers College Press, [2021] | Series: TEC series | Includes bibliographical references and index.
Identifiers: LCCN 2021022347 (print) | LCCN 2021022348 (ebook) | ISBN 9780807765722 (paperback) | ISBN 9780807765739 (hardcover) | ISBN 9780807779767 (ebook)
Subjects: LCSH: Arts in education.
Classification: LCC NX280 .H35 2021 (print) | LCC NX280 (ebook) | DDC 700.71—dc23
LC record available at https://lccn.loc.gov/2021022347
LC ebook record available at https://lccn.loc.gov/2021022348

ISBN 978-0-8077-6572-2 (paper)
ISBN 978-0-8077-6573-9 (hardcover)
ISBN 978-0-8077-7976-7 (ebook)

Printed on acid-free paper
Manufactured in the United States of America

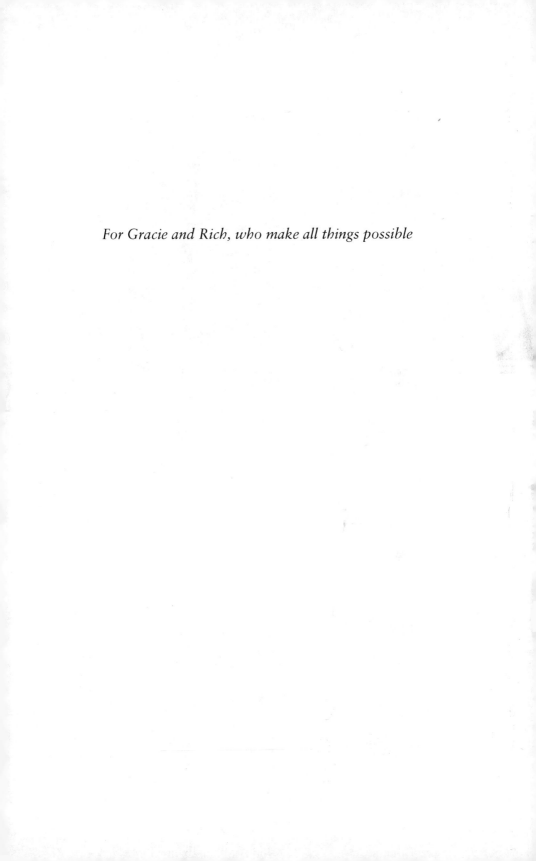

For Gracie and Rich, who make all things possible

Contents

Foreword

The arts open your heart and mind to possibilities that are limitless. They are pathways that touch upon our brains and emotions and bring sustenance to imagination. Human beings' greatest form of communication, they walk in tandem with science and play, and best describe what it is to be human.

—Jacques d'Amboise

These are the words of one of the greatest artists, educators, and evangelists for the arts that we have known. I had the extraordinary privilege of serving as Jacques d'Amboise's right hand as artistic director of National Dance Institute (NDI), the arts education organization that he founded while still a principal dancer with New York City Ballet. In the early days of NDI, we met Erica Halverson, a 4th-grader in one of NDI's dance programs.

Erica was full of energy, curiosity, and imagination, and wise beyond her years. In performance, she expressed herself with joy and confidence. When Erica joined NDI, I was a youngster myself, just out of college and focusing on my career as a performer. I signed on as a teaching artist after Jacques reached out with an offer that I thought at the time would supplement my income as a performer. Little did I know then how much my life (and Erica's!) would change, and how we would both grow from the experience of knowing Jacques.

Erica Halverson, that 4th-grader who entered our world as a young dancer, is now an artist, scholar, professor of Curriculum and Instruction at the University of Wisconsin, and founder of Whoopensocker, the arts education program that she created and continues to lead. It has been thrilling to follow her career and to know that her experience as a 9-year-old in NDI's arts-based program lit a fire that became a lifelong passion and commitment to children, the arts, and education.

Erica's aptly titled book is a must-read for all educators. In it she distills the essence of good education and makes us rethink what comprises the process of learning and effective curriculum design. Flipping the model of what success looks like in the classroom beyond test scores and content acquisition, she shines a light on the impact and transformative power of high-quality arts experiences in the life of young learners and reflects on what happens in the moment when students are engaged at the highest level, when they are given real-world reasons for working hard. It is a focus on deep learning that transfers to everything that follows in the life of a student.

I want to share two key takeaways from the book that resonated with me and which echo Jacques' vision for arts education:

The importance of risk taking: Erica speaks to the power of risk-taking as crucial for a successful classroom environment. Drawing on educational theory and practical experience, she gives us specific strategies for developing activities that facilitate sequential risk-taking. At NDI, the performative context provides the environment for risk-taking that is shared by the ensemble. Indeed, the individual child's fear of risk is diminished as steps are learned, peer-to-peer mentorship is demonstrated, and mastery of lessons lead to performance, the success of which is shared by the entire community.

Taking collective responsibility: Another lesson from Jacques' playbook that is referenced in Erica's work occurs the moment the teaching artist enters the school. Jacques taught us to take time to acknowledge everyone, from the security guard at the door to the custodian, and to make sure we connected with the principal after each class. As we begin to know the members of the school community, we encourage them to invest in the success of the program and the culminating performance itself. In this way, after weeks of rehearsal, with the principal singing in the chorus, the custodian playing the drums, and the security guard cheering from the back of the auditorium, the children feel embraced and supported, seen, and celebrated. The whole school is transformed by the experience.

I see evidence every day of how risk-taking and collective responsibility shape the lives of children who participate in the arts. Christian, for example, was a student in an NDI program. He struggled academically and socially in the traditional classroom, but in the NDI class, he was a star. During one of his dance classes, the teaching artist asked him to demonstrate a movement that he had invented, which he did, full out and with confidence. She then asked the rest of his classmates to give him feedback. The group shared positive feedback and embraced his breakthrough moment of triumph. When they finished sharing, Christian sat down next to the teacher and whispered, "All of those compliments just put the pieces of my heart back together."

As Jacques always said, "Lift your knees, look at the audience and smile, for there is only now." We are the choreographers and performers of our own lives, and this is the lesson we need to impart to our children. Give them the best, and they will become the best; dancing, singing, and telling the stories that will help them choreograph their own futures filled with creativity, empathy, possibilities, and joy.

—*Ellen Weinstein*

Acknowledgments

It took me 15 years in academia to write my first book, so this is going to read like one of those speeches at the Oscars. Feel free to have the play-off music going in your head as you read. My first arts baby, Playmakers Laboratory (née Barrel of Monkeys), was a collective effort born in the late 1990s from a small group of excited college grads who designed an artist-in-residence program that formed the basis of how I work with young people. Halena Kays, my forever partner in crime, now herself a fancy professor of directing and acting at Northwestern University, and I are forever grateful to that original group: Jonathan Mastro, Eric Silverberg, Jason Sperling, Cesar Torres, Kristie Koehler Vuocolo, and the late Jessica Martin. Thank you, and I love you. I became a better artist and teacher in those early years thanks to Roger Ainslie, Lisa Barker, Molly Brennan, Ithamar Enriquez, Charlie Farrell, Ricardo Gamboa, Luke Hatton, Oona Hatton, Rebecca Jackson-Artis, Beau Johnson, Jennifer Johnson, Tom Malinowski, Matt Miller, Tracy Repep, Geoff Rice, Joe Schupbach, Mike Spatafora, Kate Staiger, Mike Tutaj, Ryan Walters, and everyone else whose rehearsal space was also a dog-grooming place.

Being in the learning-sciences program at Northwestern University in the early 2000s was a real boon for me. I had the honor of being mentored by the great Carol D. Lee. Working on Carol's Cultural Modeling in Narrative project sparked my interest in understanding how kids' stories can function as sites of understanding learning and identity. Carol also encouraged me to look beyond my backyard, and study an arts organization that wasn't my own. As a result, my dissertation work with the About Face Youth Theatre has formed the foundation of everything I know about how young people learn to make art about the stories of their lives. A huge thank-you to Megan Carney, Eric Rosen, and the late Brian Goodman for letting me share your space, and build the basis of my work with you and the young people of AFYT.

My first project at the University of Wisconsin–Madison—a series of case studies of youth media arts organizations around the country—was made possible through a grant from the MacArthur Foundation to the Games and Professional Practice Simulations Group, which was led by world-famous sociolinguist Jim Gee and included up-and-coming scholars

Rich Halverson, David Shaffer, Kurt Squire, and Constance Steinkuehler; they encouraged me to take my insights about live performance and apply them to digital artmaking. Thanks to their generosity, I had the resources to work with graduate students on this project. I am hugely grateful to these now-tenured professors Rebecca Lowenhaupt, Alecia Magnifico, and Damiana Gibbons Pyles, medical-research librarian Michelle Bass, and instructional designers Chris Blakesley and T. J. Kalaitzidis. Many of the insights in this book were developed with these folks, and I continue to rely on Becca, Alecia, and Damiana for intellectual partnership.

In 2011, fellow artist-turned-academic Kim Sheridan asked me if I had heard anything about this Maker Movement that everyone was talking about. I had not. Thanks to her, I was introduced to a whole world of artist-engineers who were creating communities where they could design, critique, share, and experience one another's work. And Kim has been an amazing thought partner and friend since then. We have written a ton together, including work on arts education that shaped a lot of my initial thinking on what people learn in and through the arts. A lot of those ideas are reflected in this book. Our program officer at the National Science Foundation (and mentor to female learning scientists everywhere), Janet Kolodner, made it possible for us to center the arts in grants about making and the Maker Movement (NSF grants 1216994 and 1418824). I also want to acknowledge the lifelong collaborative partnerships I developed with Breanne Litts and Lisa Brahms. Breanne's intellectual partnership is central to much of what I do around making and education, and Lisa introduced me to the whole world of making in informal education, specifically, in museums and libraries. We also worked with graduate students Trevor Owens and Beau Johnson and post-docs Abby Konopasky and Lynette Priebe—and the staff at the Children's Museum of Pittsburgh. None of the studies we did were pull-off-able without this team.

I also have to give a shout-out to the team I worked with on Bubbler@MPL—the development and study of maker programs at the Madison Public Library: My research partner UW-Madison library and information sciences professor Rebekah Willett, graduate student researcher Alexandra Lakind, and the extraordinary team at the Bubbler, Trent Miller, Rebecca Millerjohn, Carlee Latimer, and Jesse Vieau. If you don't have a relationship with your public librarians, you are missing out.

My second foray into the NSF research world was the result of a 5-year collaboration with the good folks at Northcentral Technical College in Wausau, Wisconsin. The EMMET Project (NSF grant 1639915) is a true partnership between the folks on the ground working with young people in rural Wisconsin—Darren Ackley, Tim Fettig, Michael Hladilek, Vicki Jeppesen, Linda Willis, and Jenna Aderholdt—and our research team at UW. "Team Redhead"—Michael Dando, Jessie Nixon, and Andy Stoiber—collectively, made research magic happen.

I have been working for the past 3 years on the idea that collaboration is more than a means to achieve certain learning outcomes—it is an outcome of learning in the arts that we ought to value for itself. I first started talking through collaboration-as-learning-outcome with my very first Becoming a Teaching Artist class at the University of Wisconsin–Madison in 2017; I kept our collaborative class notes, and they have really shaped my thinking. Thank you to Kailea Saplan, Nuoyi Yang, and the other students in this class, for your partnership in developing these ideas. Thanks to Vishesh Kumar and Gaithri Jayathirtha for organizing a recent symposium through the International Conference of the Learning Sciences, where we collectively explored the concept of collaboration in the learning sciences, and to Breanne and Brian Gravel, for writing with me about collaboration-as-outcome.

The UW-Madison Arts Collaboratory (Arts Collab) Team is my current touchstone for all things arts and learning. Thanks to the Arts Collab, which now includes co-directors Faisal Abdu'Allah, Kate, Yorel Lashley, Mariah LeFeber, and the indomitable Stephanie Richards, for their fellowship. The Arts Collab houses all of our community-arts outreach programs, including my current arts education child, Whoopensocker. We have also created a research lab that gives us space to think about how our community-arts programs impact the learning lives of kids. One person I would not be able to do my current research without is Caitlin Martin, who ensures that our work understanding out-of-school time youth arts organizations is focused and productive.

Whoopensocker is a big part of my current story and thinking, so I rely heavily on this family to keep me sane. The Whoopensocker family includes my work spouses, Amanda Farrar and Jessica Jane Witham. You are the engine to my steering wheel. You are the goats to my totes. I am forever grateful to Beau Johnson, for finding the word *Whoopensocker*. When he, Amanda, and I were first dreaming up what Barrel of Monkeys 2.0 could look like, he came to us, having scoured the *Dictionary of American Regional English* for good Wisconsin words. He hit on a winner. A very special "whoop it up" to the members of Whoopensocker who dedicate themselves to creativity with young people in Madison! I was going to name you all, but the book would be over then. (Andy Stoiber, you have been with us this whole time, so you get an extra "whoop it up!")

The writing of this book would not have been possible without my partnership with Jenny Price. She has the gentlest way of saying, "I have no idea what you're talking about" that I have experienced. Rich Halverson is my editor for everything in life; this book is no different. He had the hardest job of all—telling me I wasn't finished writing when I desperately wanted to be.

The beautiful cover art and line drawings in the book are a result of a collaboration with Lyra Evans. I am grateful to Maureen Janson Heintz for the author photo that appears on the book's back cover.

I would not have ever gone into a career at the intersection of the arts and education without the incredible arts educators who brought me in and nurtured me throughout my life. Jacques d'Amboise, Ellen Weinstein, and the National Dance Institute taught me how to be an artist and an empathetic human. Thank you for inviting me to the SWAT Team all the way back in 1984, when I knew nothing about either art or empathy. Finally, like many of you, I had inspirational teachers along the way who encouraged, pushed, and inspired my love for all things artmaking. I had the world's best elementary school music teacher—Barbara Ames—and high school music teacher—Campbell Austin. And, when I got to college, my acting teacher Mary Poole and professor of creative drama and children's theater Rives Collins. I am here because of the professional arts teachers in my life throughout my education who were also invested in making the arts a core part of who I am as a person.

Introduction
Something Extraordinary of Its Kind

Whoopensocker is a community-arts outreach program in Madison, Wisconsin, and I am its self-proclaimed mayor. From the *Dictionary of American Regional English, whoopensocker* is an old Wisconsin word that refers to a special version of whatever noun you are talking about. If you've spent time in the upper Midwest, you would not be surprised to hear someone say, "Oh yah, we had a whoopensocker of a party last night. It was a real good time!" The word is simultaneously silly and local. In our artist-in-residence program, teaching artists work in community with elementary school students and classroom teachers on creative expression through writing, storytelling, improvisation, and theater performance. We spend seven weekly sessions working with an entire grade of students to produce stories across a range of storytelling formats. The climax of the program is a performance by professional artists that features a selection of the kids' stories. We perform during the day for the entire school and then again in the evenings for families and communities who bear witness to the genius of our young writers. This program embodies all of the good ideas that I have ever had, heard, or read about how arts practices shape learning and teaching.

In this whoopensocker of a program, we engage in telling, adapting, and performing stories. This is the core of what we do, and it is the core of any design for an arts-based learning environment. Telling stories looks a lot of different ways. It looks like a teaching artist crouched over a giant piece of lined paper fielding suggestions from nine 3rd-graders about what to name the unicorn that is the hero of their story (spoiler alert—his name is Sparkletoes). It also looks like a trio of kids collaboratively writing a short play, where each of them scribes lines and stage directions in their own notebooks, so that they can later perform these plays for their peers. It also looks like a kid sitting by themselves under a desk in the back corner of the room, creating comic-book panels illustrating why kids should be allowed to make comics in school.

Adapting stories also comes in many different flavors. We are constantly adapting in the classroom. The 3rd-graders who wrote about the unicorn portray Sparkletoes and his friends and foes for the rest of their class. Kids read their stories out loud, as teaching artists improvise their way through getting lost in the mall or driving from Madison to Chicago for cousins' birthday parties. Adaptation also happens in the rehearsal room where professional performers flex their artist muscles by bringing in tools and skills from their lives outside of Whoopensocker. Modern dance choreography, reggae music, and shadow puppetry are all regular components of our group of artists working together. And when we use our artistic tools, we only do so if it lines up with the author's intention. We ask ourselves, our fellow teaching artists, and the classroom teachers whether our adaptation decisions honor what the kids were trying to express.

Our performances of youth-authored stories simultaneously push on the norms for representation and honor the kids' voices. The ensemble is purposefully diverse; we aim for kids to see themselves onstage and to subvert assumptions about who holds power in a given situation. We will cast a 17-year-old African American ensemble member to play President Barack Obama even as the character is teaching a group of kids, all played by performers ages 35–60. When it turns out that this ensemble member also went to the elementary school we are performing in, well, he becomes a local celebrity. The Whoopensocker model is the foundation of my story for how the arts can transform education.

The age of accountability in education is losing its momentum. Education is in a time of profound change. We are increasingly aware of how learning outside of school provides life-giving opportunities for our most vulnerable kids. The arts—dance, theater, music, the visual arts, and the digital and design arts—offer us a way to reimagine what good learning and teaching are and how to design learning environments that work for all kids. The COVID-19 pandemic shut down schools and exposed ever-present inequities in education. And though it has been heart-wrenching for teachers, students, and families, the disruption has also offered us the opportunity to fundamentally rethink what education can be. Gloria Ladson-Billings has called for a "hard reset" on education and for us to fundamentally reconsider the kind of human beings we want to produce (2021). In this book, I will describe how the arts can save education by providing new models for learning that embrace the social, cultural, and historical assets that kids bring to the classroom. I will also share how an arts-based approach to teaching focuses on risk-taking as the most important aspect of a successful classroom. I offer a framework that leverages how arts practitioners do their work to design learning experiences for all subject areas. Throughout, I use my own arts organization, Whoopensocker, as a model for how to reframe learning as acts of metacognitive representation, identity development, and collaboration—and lots and lots of joy.

Before we get started, I want to make a few things clear. This is not a book about arts education. There are many fine books on how to teach the arts both in and out of schools, and I encourage you to read them all! What I am offering is something more. I use arts practices to fundamentally rethink what learning outcomes we should value, how we should teach, and how to design learning environments and experiences that can serve all kids. In my world, we are not teaching and learning the arts—the arts are teaching and learning. I will be using the terms *arts education*, *arts practices*, and *artmaking* throughout this book. Across all of these, I am referring to the arts as a collective set of disciplines where people produce things. Those things can be physical artifacts, like clay pots or short films, or they can be ephemeral performances, like a music concert or improvised scene. Many of my examples are drawn from the performing arts, because I have been performing my whole life. But this argument is inclusive of all forms where creative expression is involved. Okay, on with the show.

WE BUILT THIS CITY . . . ON EDUCATIONAL RESEARCH

My approach to describing the power of telling, adapting, and performing stories for Whoopensocker's citizens and for all those who participate in arts practices begins with three theoretical perspectives on education research: cognitive science, the new literacies, and culturally sustaining pedagogies. *Cognitive science* is the ground floor where education researchers define thinking, knowing, and learning. The field has examined knowing and learning from the cognitive perspective—what's going on "inside peoples' heads"—and from the sociocultural perspective—in the social, cultural, and historical interactions that are characteristic of the way people engage with one another in particular contexts (How People Learn II, 2018). Specifically, I'm interested in the branch of cognitive science that describes thinking as distributed—stretched across people, tools, and time (Hutchins, 1996). Best practices in the arts connect directly to social, cultural, and historical models of cognition, and show up all throughout Whoopensocker City.

The new literacies—what could be "new" about literacy? Don't you just mean reading and writing? Actually, no. Folks who work in the study of literacy now understand being literate as ways of knowing, doing, being, seeing, valuing, and believing, all of which are embedded in the things we consume and the things we create (Lankshear & Knobel, 2011). In this way, artmaking *is* a literacy practice aimed at communicating thoughts and ideas to real-life audiences.

Culturally sustaining pedagogies is a foundational set of commitments in education research that teaching starts by connecting kids' worlds and valuing what they bring to a learning environment (Paris & Alim, 2017). This is of the utmost importance, if our goal is to work with all kids. Some people also call this "asset pedagogies," meaning starting with what kids bring to learning, as opposed to a deficit orientation, which focuses on what kids lack. The arts are a natural fit for cultural relevance, and this scholarship has been foundational to my understanding of how artmakers (young and old) shape what good learning looks like.

Arts practices where people learn to make things serve as a bridge across all these big ideas in education research—cognitive science, the new literacies, and culturally relevant and culturally sustaining pedagogies. Cognitive science describes learning *by* making, where people use available tools and resources to work through difficult ideas, while the new literacies focuses on learning *in* making, that is, learning in the act of designing representations (McLean & Rowsell, 2021). In both framings, making things is an opportunity to capture, represent, and share issues of culture and power (Barajás-Lopez & Bang, 2018). So, it is more than just making things; we make with and through a critical lens where "critical" implies attention to the role of power, inequality, and marginalization in discussions of teaching and learning. Creating artistic representations that feature youth experiences, perspectives, and values brings together these three foundational education theories around what kids are learning to know, do, and be.

LEARNING IN AND THROUGH THE ARTS

Now, like Missy Elliott circa 2002, I'll put that thing down, flip it, and reverse it. Instead of using education research ideas to explain the arts, I use the arts to explain how we ought to reimagine learning. It may seem funny to say that learning needs to be reimagined, but most of what is wrong with how we construct education reform is the assumption that learning outcomes exist independently of the learning process. Schools, researchers, and policymakers are open to changing the methods of getting to the outcomes, but, for the most part, the underlying ideas of what counts as learning does not change: Learning is a decontextualized demonstration of standardized content and a fixed set of "basic" skills. I offer a rethinking of what counts with three core learning outcomes of arts-based learning.

People who make art learn to *create representations*, which is the foundational process for being a successful student across disciplines. Just as a picture can be a representation of a scene or a feeling, an answer to a question in an algebra class is a representation of a learner's understanding of a concept. The arts require learners to master the representational tools of a medium. Learners typically create many representations that build on each other in the artmaking process. We call this sequence a "representational trajectory," which traces a path from initial idea to final artwork. Following this trajectory creates many opportunities to assess progress (Halverson, 2013). A representational trajectory also supports language development as learners receive critique and create new representations that reflect new language moves in the medium (Soep, 2006). The arts offer opportunities for kids to engage in hybrid-language practices, where young artists build representations in multiple languages, depending on what they want to communicate, and learn to make explicit choices about when to draw on which language (Machado & Hartman, 2019). Focusing on representations to document the process of learning also allows us to track the process and product of creative production and to evaluate the innovative potential of ideas (Kaufman & Sternberg, 2010a).

Artmaking centers *identity* as a process of experimenting with and becoming and as a product of creating, doing, and enacting. The art itself is also a representation of identity. It provides evidence of how learners understand who they are and demonstrates how they share their understanding with the world. Rather than considering identity as fixed content, identity in artmaking is a process of experimenting with new ways of doing and being. In making art, young people try on different selves, both desired and feared; these acts of "exploring possible selves" can be done without long-term consequences (Markus & Nurius, 1986). Importantly, these explorations can be individualistic or collectivistic, so a range of identity processes are supported across different cultural communities (Triandis, 2001).

In the arts, *collaboration* is not only a condition of the work, it is also an important outcome. People learn to collaborate through participating in arts practices. Even solo activities draw on the collective knowledge built into the techniques and tools of generations of artmakers. Artmaking as learning shifts our understanding of collaboration from a tool for getting individuals to learn to a legitimate product of participating in a learning process.

When we engage in artmaking, we learn to make representations, to experiment with and produce identities, and to collaborate. This contrasts with the current model of fixed content and skill outcomes of school-based learning. These three outcomes serve as the foundation for how we can remake learning for the next generation of schooling.

IMPROV AS THE MODEL FOR GOOD TEACHING

Adopting new learning outcomes means we need a new way of teaching. Gone are teaching to the test and ensuring that all students produce identical outcomes on the same age-graded schedule. Instead, I will argue that teaching should be modeled on improvisation, a genre of performance across music, theater, and dance where people spontaneously draw on what is known to create their own emergent and collaborative teaching opportunities. Improv has four key features, which I adapt from Tina Fey and her memoir *Bossypants* (2011). Tina (I like to call her Tina, so I can pretend she's my BFF) identifies four rules of improv that will help guide our understanding of good teaching:

1. *Always say, "Yes!"* When we improvise with one another, it is crucial that we always affirm what our partner gives us. This does not

mean we can't say the word "no"; it means that we can't pretend as if the other person didn't offer us something. If I start a scene by saying, "I have a hand growing out of my head"—the only thing you can't say is, "No, you don't." You might respond, "That's terrifying!" Or, "How did it get there?" Or, "High five!" But you must acknowledge what I've said and incorporate it into your response. The same goes for teaching. Taking an improvisational stance means acknowledging that what students bring into the classroom is the foundation of any learning experience.

2. ***Actually, say, "Yes, and . . . "*** As teachers, we go beyond affirmation toward working with students to build new ideas from our existing ones. In this way, learning is a productive dialogue among the people and tools within a learning environment. The "and" reminds us that keeping the interaction going is the key to inviting learners to create new rounds of representations.

3. ***Make statements.*** When you know the answer to a question, or you have a specific direction you would like students to go in, it is okay to say so. Make a clear statement about what you think, or what you feel and that will move the interaction forward. Imagine listening to an improv jazz band when no musician steps forward to take a turn as a soloist. The piece stagnates, musicians get stuck, and audiences get bored. Knowing when to take the lead in a learning environment is a marker of effective improvisational teaching.

4. ***Turn mistakes into opportunities.*** This is a great way to engage students' prior knowledge in learning something new. If a concept is unfamiliar and intimidating, students are likely to resist engaging with it. Encouraging participants to engage with whatever they have to say gets the interaction cycle happening—if the contribution is way off base, teachers and other participants can build on it to create a meaningful context. Any contribution, including mistakes, can advance the discussion. Even acts of resistance can be turned by improvisational teaching from "not" doing into ways of connecting with the learning goals.

Together, these four rules demonstrate that improv-as-teaching is fundamentally about scaffolding risk-taking. Scaffolding, because risk-taking is not something people are all that willing to do of their own accord, especially when they're with people they don't know or trust and when they think there are high stakes involved. And risk-taking, because no one can learn if they are not willing to be wrong, and you won't be wrong if you don't take a risk. This goes for teachers as well as students, anyone who is engaged in the act of learning together. Improv invites teachers to think about and expand these important steps of inviting participants into a new learning space and to sustain the kinds of engagement that lead to creative learning.

REIMAGINING CURRICULUM THROUGH THE LENS OF DESIGN

The third leg of the "how the arts can save education" stool is the design of the learning environment. An artmaking perspective on the learning environment focuses on design as a process for creating, where educators customize to choose and support a curriculum that works for their context and their students. While learning is a naturally occurring phenomenon, learning *something* requires design (Wenger, 1998). Design allows us to set the rules of engagement, so that creativity can happen more readily within the constraints of the designed environment. We call these rules "design principles," and I offer three arts-based design principles that structure learning environments for representation, identity, and collaboration.

Design Principle 1: Conceive, Represent, Share. The best way to teach something new is to take an idea or concept, represent it using the tools of a medium, and share it with an audience who has a reason to care about what you're saying. This principle follows the telling, adapting, performing model we use in Whoopensocker. Telling is like the "conceive" stage—it means coming up with the focal idea, concept, or story to share with learners. "Represent" means creating a new form of the idea, with the tools of the medium you are working in, and exploring how the affordances of the tools can help communicate your idea. "Share" is the process of introducing the representation with learners. It invites teachers to reflect on how, with whom, and in what context student work will be shared as a core part of the learning process. Collectively, "conceive, represent, share" is the process of productive teaching and learning in an artmaking learning space.

Design Principle 2: Assessment is Authentic, Embedded, and Constant. Assessment is built into the structure of any artmaking learning environment. It is embedded throughout the production cycle and in the resulting products. In the arts, we use critique as a mechanism for assessment during the process (Hetland et al., 2013), and we rely on sequenced representations to holistically capture process at the end (Tseng, 2016). To assess products as outcomes of learning, we rely on external audiences to provide feedback in the form of reactions, suggestions, and recognition. All of these assessment mechanisms are authentic, that is, seamlessly embedded in the "conceive, represent, share" cycle, so no external measures have to be introduced. In a good artmaking learning environment, assessment is happening all the time as a helpful component of the learning process.

Design Principle 3: Ideas First, Tools Second. New learners in arts-based learning spaces can get overwhelmed by the range of tools available. What does this button do? Where am I supposed to stand? What form of rhyming and meter should I use? Instead, I have found that we learn to use new tools best when we need them to accomplish a task around ideas that we care about. It is harder to memorize math equations without needing to use them to solve a problem than it is to have a problem, and then try to learn how a particular equation helps you to solve it. "Ideas first, tools second" means that we take a just-in-time approach to working with tools and materials, offering formal lessons on complicated tools only when learners need them to develop their ideas (Gee, 2007).

THE ARTS TAKE CENTER STAGE

The ideas involved in artmaking sound to many teachers, parents, and learners like precisely what should be happening every day in our schools. Why haven't our schools already realized an arts-based vision for learning, teaching, and the design of learning environments? Why don't our schools look more like artmaking spaces? I present a play, in three acts, that describes how we have been caught up in a vicious cycle of identifying the ways that the arts can solve persistent problems in education, only to have reform efforts snap back to the traditional practices and measures of schooling, and dilute and discard the intrinsic value of arts practices.

   Act I: The Accountability Machine. In the opening act of our play, we meet the antagonist: an accountability movement that positions our kids as "at risk," because they trail their peers around the world in test scores that are designed to measure achievements and future life prospects. As a result, we narrowed the purpose of schooling to focus almost exclusively on test scores as evidence of learning. As Elliott Eisner lamented, "achievement has triumphed over inquiry" (2004, p. 3). Our protagonists: arts educators everywhere. In the early years, they adapted and survived by providing evidence that the arts could act in service of these narrowed outcomes. When arts programming continued to be cut, our heroes called for more research and practice to establish the intrinsic value of the arts for learners.

   Act II: The Rise of STEM. The arts were not the only subjects that suffered at the hands of the Accountability Machine. STEM, a potential love interest for our hero, entered the conversation in the 2000s by using a global competitiveness argument to prioritize science, technology, engineering, and mathematics (Mejias et al., 2021). STEM advocates argued that a new path out of our "rising tide of mediocrity" was to invest in initiatives that offered STEM access for underrepresented students, as well as teacher and curricular development. Romance was on the horizon when we put the arts in STEM to make STEAM. This romance could blossom—the arts and STEM share many ways of knowing, doing, and being that stretch across both disciplines, including exploration, meaning-making, and critiquing (Bevan et al., 2019). Some even say that STEM and the arts managed to have a baby that they named the Maker Movement (Halverson & Peppler, 2018). But alas, this couple bends toward the fate of a mid-life crisis; all too often, the arts become tokenized in service of STEM aims and purposes in the same ways that the arts were used to support reading and math accountability. Still, focusing on making as acts of culturally sustaining STEAM production that value the social, cultural, and historical assets that kids bring to their learning environments is our best hope for keeping this relationship alive (Ryoo & Calabrese Barton, 2018).

Act III: Putting the Arts at the Center. In the final act, we find inspiration in the informal learning environments that have blossomed all around our star-crossed lovers. Informal learning environments have a lot to teach schools about how to value young peoples' social, cultural, and historical resources as a way to create engaging, dynamic, and effective systems of teaching and learning. Perhaps more importantly, they bring the excellence and beauty of young people and their worlds into what they make. Often, these acts of creativity stand in contrast with the experience of artmakers in schools. Artmaking can be simultaneously an act of resistance to, and a triumph over, a system that tells young people that they are not worthwhile.

TAKING THE ARTS TO SCHOOL

Our schools are in desperate need of new approaches to teaching and learning. Artmaking spaces provide new approaches in the form of time-tested, proven practices for learning that draw on learners' identities and communities and allow makers to take control of their own learning. I will not overwhelm you with specific arts practices that require years of expertise to achieve competence. Instead, I want to identify the pathways for ready access to arts practices that provide deep and meaningful connections to big ideas across disciplines. And though an educator's mastery of an art form is not required to transform learning outcomes, teaching strategies, or the design of learning environments, collaboration with those who do have expertise is essential. My recommendations come in the form of three big ideas:

Big Idea 1: Honor Risk-Taking as a Core Feature of Teaching and Learning. Educators must take time and space to scaffold risk for all members of the learning community. This includes educators who are coming to arts-based practices for the first time. No one is prepared to learn, much less engage in a production cycle of conceiving, representing, and sharing, without a willingness to take risks. Modeling how to take risks, and how to respond in ways that keep the flow of ideas going, is the first Big Idea of building the arts into everyday teaching and learning.

Big Idea 2: Embrace Identity and Representation as Core Ideas, but Do Not Mistake One for the Other. Representation and identity are two primary outcomes of participation in arts practices. And while young people often use artistic representation to explore and share their identities, it is important not to romanticize creative expression (Sefton-Green, 2000). People use the arts to experiment with who they are and who they might become and to test out new concepts and ideas. We need to allow these expressions to live in a playful space of experimentation for testing out new ways of being. We want to be careful not to define makers by what they create and not to conflate the art people produce with their understanding of who they are.

Big Idea 3: Take Collective Responsibility. You do not have to do this alone! All arts-based learning experiences are distributed across a learning ecology that includes formal and informal educators, young people, and a host of analog and virtual tools and resources (Barron, 2006). The knowledge built into the tools and techniques of artmaking are a kind of asynchronous collaboration with prior generations of artists, and the practices of conceiving, representing, sharing and assessing are actively synchronous collaborative activities. Becoming a participant in this ongoing artmaking process allows you to take your part in keeping the conversation rolling.

I can't promise you that embracing an arts-based vision for learning, teaching, and design will be easy. But the stories, examples and the ideas that follow will help you see how my colleagues and I used the arts and artmaking to bring joy to classrooms, and to lead the way toward a more equitable and just educational future for all.

CHAPTER 1

Whoop It Up! Sock It to Me!

It is the middle of March 2019. Spring break is looming on the horizon, and, if you haven't ever been to Madison, Wisconsin, that horizon is gray, cold, and wet. It is hard to find joy, when the temperature never gets quite high enough to take off your scarf, except in a public school building where the heat is so intense and dry that the liquid in your water bottle evaporates before you can drink it. But there is excitement coming from inside the auditorium at Imagination[1] Elementary School. It is Whoopensocker show day, which means every student is filing into the room to watch a group of professional artists from across the city perform stories written by 3rd-graders from their school.

This is the fourth year that Whoopensocker has been at Imagination, so older kids have already had their stories performed in past years, and some of the younger kids have seen past shows, or have siblings who participated in the program. The Whoopensocker actors are already onstage, warming up by playing the exact games (Three Things! Zip Zap Zop!) they played with kids when they were teaching artists in their classrooms. Kids cry out, "There's Andi!" Or "Hi, Janine!" And there's even an unexpected hug between a 4th-grader and a Whoopensocker teaching artist from last year who is just there to watch the performance. Amanda, the director of this show, calls for attention from the stage with our signature, "Whoop it up!" Nearly the whole room replies, "Sock it to me!" They know the show is about to begin.

The show represents the culmination of 6 weeks of artist-in-residence work in 3rd-grade classrooms. Whoopensocker has been bringing teaching artists into classrooms in Madison since 2015. Our mission is to get kids—*all* of the kids—to express themselves creatively and to see their stories, poems, arguments, and plays adapted and performed by professional artists. When we enter into a residency agreement with a school, we ensure that we can work with the whole grade, regardless of the kids' perceived ability status. As they say in the best Pixar movie of all time, *Ratatouille*, "Anyone can cook!" Once a week, a team of teaching artists leads 90 minutes of classroom activities designed to inspire and stretch kids to write, draw, perform, or dictate stories around a theme. In the first week, we introduce our own make-believe world, Whoopensocker City, and we walk through

Whoopensocker Show Day at Imagination Elementary School

the basic components of a fictional story. After that, we choose a particular inspiration for storytelling: writing stories from pictures, true stories, playwriting, and arguments designed to "Make a change!" Each theme serves as the foundation for the skills and habits of mind we want learners to develop. In the final week, we collect the stories kids write throughout the residency and share them, so they can adapt and perform each other's works.

WHOOPENSOCKER (N.): SOMETHING EXTRAORDINARY OF ITS KIND

Calling our program Whoopensocker and creating a special place known as Whoopensocker City, where the program happens, is an intentional choice. It allows us to create a whole world that we can co-occupy during our residency time. Teaching artists, kids, and classroom teachers all become part of Whoopensocker City as a way to acknowledge that we are doing something different than we typically do in school, but that all school people are welcome. Principals often visit Whoopensocker City. They come to classrooms and adjudicate arguments about whether pets should be allowed in schools (a favorite debate during "make a change" day). They make cameos in performances, usually as themselves, but sometimes dressed up as other characters. These are still school days, but they are whoopensocker days.

Whoopensocker City allows us to create a classroom space where all students can express themselves freely through writing and performance, as individuals and as collaborators. Throughout our time, we tell stories in a variety of formats. We play theater games and introduce the day's theme in a whole group. On playwriting day, teaching artists solicit suggestions for characters and settings, and then improvise through a short dialogue with actions that pairs of kids can volunteer to reenact for the class. We also do a lot of story writing in small groups. Each classroom has enough teaching artists to keep the teacher–student ratio to around 8:1. This allows us to split the class among the teaching artists, and work in small groups to create and then perform stories for the rest of the class. For example, on True Story Day, teaching artists tell the story of something that really happened, and then help the students in their groups create a performance of that story for everyone else. There is also a lot of time during the residency for kids to work alone or in pairs telling their own stories. We encourage them to use whatever media of storytelling is most available to them—writing, drawing/cartooning, talking out loud for another person to transcribe—in order to best express themselves.

By 3rd grade, we have found that many kids are worried about "doing it right." Doing it right seems to include correct spelling and punctuation and the appropriate number of sentences or words. In Whoopensocker City, we empower kids to write in whatever way makes sense for them and for their ideas. Our standard line when it comes to these concerns is, "We are really good at reading spelling, so don't worry about us." It's not that we don't care about spelling, it's more that we don't want the right form to get in the way of expression, creativity, and joy. Whoopensocker teaching artists then team up with classroom teacher partners to use story writing as a pathway for moving their students toward mastering standard spelling and grammar practices. Whoopensocker kids also write in whatever language is most comfortable for them. In Madison, there are a fair number of 3rd-graders for whom writing in Spanish is much easier than writing in English. This works for us, since the schools we work in typically have bilingual resource teachers in the classrooms, and we try to have at least one Spanish speaker on our teaching-artist team. There are also kids who speak and practice languages at home other than English, and they are eager to try out hybrid language practices. We have seen stories that have components of Mandarin, Arabic, Hmong, or Russian; most of these stories represent a mix of kids' current expertise in both their home language and academic English.

Every residency—usually, an entire grade of anywhere between 70–95 students—produces hundreds of stories. The Whoopensocker team collects the notebooks that we have given kids to write their stories, and we read *everything*. That's right; we sit around a giant table—always with snacks—and we go through every journal. Every kid gets feedback from two of us, in the form of within-story notes and a short letter at the front of their journal, remarking on a particular memory from the residency that stood out to that teaching artist. We encourage kids to write everything down and tell them that they can fold over the pages that contain stories they don't want anyone to read. Occasionally that happens, and we respect their privacy. Though we don't see kids in that final week of work, we pay our teaching artists for their time, and we think of this feedback session as a critically important part of our model.

The other thing that happens in the final week is that we start to identify which pieces from the residency's oeuvre[2] we want to include in our totally original vaudeville-style sketch show that we premiere at that school for the authors, their peers, and the school community. Many of our teaching artists are also performers—musicians, actors, circus artists, MCs, dancers—and every residency culminates with a group of performers creating and sharing an hour-long show comprised entirely of kids' stories. The overall aesthetic for the show is what I refer to as A Charlie Brown Christmas. That tree that Charlie Brown buys might look sad, but it's real, and with a little love from the rest of the kids, it comes to life as the beautiful symbol of togetherness that it's meant to be. Just like Charlie Brown and his friends, our performances are simple and evocative, and everything the kids say is taken seriously. The Whoopensocker YouTube channel (https://www.youtube.com/c/Whoopensocker) has some of our favorite performances on it; feel free to put down this book, get lost in the rabbit hole of Whoop videos, and come back tomorrow.

The Whoopensocker company performance is where everything comes together. Each 60-minute show highlights about 20 student-authored stories, told in short 1–4 minute bursts of pure creativity. We aim to include as many student writers in each show as possible, and, before each piece, the writers are called out by name in front of the whole audience to recognize their contributions. Any one show is likely to contain Broadway belting, a Drake rap, a performance art piece told with no words, and a young banana who pretends to be sick so her mom doesn't make her go to school. Musical numbers such as "I Love Harrison Ford and You Can't Tell Me No!" and the retelling of the true story "When I Broke My Arm" help students see the power of performing stories in front of a real audience.

TELLING STORIES, ADAPTING STORIES, AND PERFORMING STORIES

Whoopensocker is designed around the cycle of telling, adapting, and performing stories; this process is the at core of many arts-based programs that work with young people on creative production (Halverson, 2007). The process involves a model of literacy-as-communication focused on the development and sharing of creative work. The cycle begins with the stories as written by students. We use all of our pedagogical tricks to set up activities for students to find a comfortable lane to express themselves through storytelling. Adapting stories happens alongside telling. We use group activities, with clear roles for students and teaching artists, that show students how literacy is as much about sharing and collaborating as it is about spelling and grammar. Finally, performing stories validates student ideas and allows the authors to see how their work looks through the eyes and actions of professional performers with real audiences.

Let me share an example of the telling, adapting, performing cycle in action. During Week 3 of the Whoopensocker residency, we tell personal stories. The day starts with teaching artists telling their own stories to small groups, then acting out our stories for the rest of the class. I am fond of telling the story of when I gave birth to my daughter. Someone always wants to play my New York Jewish mother who announces herself in the delivery room midway through my labor, looks shocked by the medical equipment, and then, promptly, gets sent out of the room without another word. There are also inanimate objects in the story—a shower, a heart monitor, a post-surgery giant heat lamp—these provide great opportunities for kids to perform who don't want to speak but are eager to participate physically in the performance. Once we perform the group stories from teaching artists, the kids write their own true stories. We always leave time at the end for the kids to read their stories out loud as the teaching artists improvise a performance. This is a sneaky way to get kids to (1) read their story out loud, (2) read loudly and clearly, and (3) value the kids and the people in their lives by embodying them in performance.

The stories teaching artists tell are based on things that have happened in our lives, so for kids who have struggled with "making stuff up," this week can be inspiring. Over the years we have learned that whatever kinds of stories the teaching artists tell will be the kinds of stories we hear from the kids. If a teaching artist tells a story about the time they got lost in the mall when they were young, we will get a bunch of "when I got lost" stories. We once got a whole series of "when I forgot my pants" stories because two of us accidentally both told stories about a time when we forgot to wear pants in public during the summer. What are the odds? Well, given how many kids *also* had stories about forgetting their pants, apparently, the odds are pretty good.

Injury stories are also common. So many of us have fallen off our bikes, or tripped on something, cut our lip, and had to go to the emergency room to get it stitched up. One particular injury story—"When I Broke My Arm"—came from Cameron, who had been pretty quiet through the first 2-and-a-half weeks of the program. He seemed close with some of the kids who definitely loved to perform and be seen, but Cameron was a bit reserved. On True Story Day, he wrote this:

The monkey bars terrify Cameron in our adaptation of "When I Broke My Arm."

"When I Broke My Arm"

One day when I was on a monkey bars on the highest one and fall and
I broke my arm my mom take me to the hospital they gave me a cast.
My arm was broke for three days. I went home the third day. Now
I'm scared to go on monkey bars again in my life. Theres this day my
mom said are you ok I said no it hurts. When it got off I was ok now
I'm scared of the monkey bars. So now I don't want to go outside to
the monkey bars. My mom and me went outside on the monkey bars.
My mom came to the monkey bars she helped me and I made it then
the monkey bars. I said I can make it it was so fun.
THE END [3]

When he had finished writing and showed it to me, I asked if he was
willing to read it out loud—loud enough for me and my co-teaching artist,
Brian, to hear, so that we could improvise our way through a performance
of it for the class. He agreed and read with clarity and confidence—so much
confidence that he would return in subsequent weeks to the practice of reading his stories out loud and having his friends act them out.

In the public performance life of this story, it has become a Whoopensocker favorite. It has been performed multiple times—first at the school
show, then again at our end-of-the-year extravaganza where we choose a
few stories from every school to perform at a professional theater space. In

our adaptation, the monkey bars are a character, played by two performers holding long poles; they are menacing and out to get the kid. The menace is only in the kid's head though, and at the end, when he overcomes his fear, they turn out to be a perfectly nice, anthropomorphized object. The two kids who gossip about our hero's fate and their jealousy over him getting to have a cast, because he broke his arm, is also a delightful addition.

TELLING STORIES

Every Idea is a Good Idea

It is Day 1 of our Whoopensocker residency at Imagination Elementary. We have not yet settled into the routine of knowing who will push whose buttons, who will run off to write under a table as soon as they get the chance, and who will permanently attach themselves to teaching artist Amanda R. who, a student once told me, looked "just like Princess Jasmine, only prettier!" As teaching artists, we meet in a small room off the school library to plan how we're going to spread ourselves across the 70-plus 3rd-graders at the school. There are typically three classrooms of kids, and this year the classroom teachers have put the kids into mixed-classroom groups. We've worked with these teachers before, so they know what to expect from us. They have put the kids into a mellow group, a rambunctious group, and a group that is already super enthusiastic about writing and performing. I take the rambunctious group with co-teaching artist Brian, who has just returned from performing in a national tour of a musical to do some directing and teaching in town. I *love* when I get to be in a room full of 3rd-graders whom teachers see as "rambunctious." They are often the most enthusiastic about performing but the most challenging to get to work together. And the classroom teachers we are partnering with are simultaneously curious and amused by what we will do to work successfully in the room.

Today, our mission is to get the class to embrace the Whoopensocker Five Agreements. These are the foundation of our collective work together, the way we set up what it means to be in community. We set up the agreements under the banner of Whoopensocker City, the place that is created inside each classroom that includes teaching artists, classroom teachers, and (of course) all the kids. When we are in Whoopensocker City, we structure all of our interactions around the agreements. Originally, we called these agreements "rules," but quickly realized that this framing felt like we were creating a city ordinance, rather than coming together to build a new learning community. We present these agreements and then ask every kid, in a small group, to recite the following: "I agree to these agreements that we have agreed upon in agreeing to work together." Then, they approach the written agreements posted on the wall and sign their names, which remain visible throughout our time together.

Whoopensocker Agreements

Every idea is a good idea.
Support each other's ideas.
Respect yourself and others.
Keep the peace.
Respect the magic sign.

All five of these agreements are simultaneously challenging and rewarding, with 22 of the 3rd grade's most rambunctious kiddos.

In the Beginning, There Was "Yes, And . . . " If you ever go to any acting or improv class, the first thing you will learn is the importance of saying yes, and. This is my top priority for kids working with Whoopensocker: that they should say yes. "Yes!" to themselves, to their own instincts and ideas, to the ideas of others, and to what can come out of taking our collective ideas to create something new and magical and strange. "No, but . . . " chills interaction immediately and makes participants withdraw, or become defensive. "Yes, and . . . " on the other hand, gives us permission to build on each other's ideas, to take what someone is giving, and make a collective new thing. Saying "yes, and . . . " is also the primary move for good teaching; it is *the* way to create a classroom where kids can share what they know, take risks, and learn new things. "Yes, and . . . " builds on what we know about how people learn, and it is how the arts can show the way for incorporating creativity throughout teaching practice.

In Whoopensocker, working with a group of kids to understand "yes, and . . ." gets you a long way toward the first three agreements. "Every idea is a good idea" is mostly about not censoring yourself. By 3rd grade, many kids have developed the notion that their own ideas are no good, that they are not creative, or that there is an expected right answer and whatever they will say is not it. We spend a lot of Whoopensocker writing time just getting kids to express their first thought. "Support each other's ideas" extends "yes, and . . . " to collaborators. It is not easy to accept someone else's brainstorm and bridge it with your own, especially if you are 8 and working with a large group of other 8-year-olds. But getting kids to see the joy in riffing off of one another is one of the great victories of creating together over time. "Respect yourself and others" is a reminder of the first two agreements but bears repeating, because knowing how to be a human among other humans is hard. It's hard for adults, and it's hard for kids. We make it a goal of collaborative creation to finish out our time with an emphasis on self-respect and respect for each other and what we make.

The other two agreements are more about having the kind of learning environment where we can all work successfully. "Keep the peace" is our way of establishing that we can perform together, but we can't use this time as an excuse to get overly physical, so that someone gets hurt. We spend time at the beginning of each session creating personal force fields that prevent us from actually touching one another. We practice "force-field high-fives"—high-fiving without touching but with a mimed force-field shock that sends two hands vibrating away from one another. We also stage "force-field lightsaber battles"—simulated lightsaber jousts where the imaginary lightsabers can touch but bodies cannot. This is a way to remind ourselves that we can play without harm. As the great Paul Rudd says in the classic film *Anchorman,* "60% of the time, it works every time." We do not succeed entirely in keeping kids from touching; in fact, with permission, we sometimes make performance pieces that require physical contact. But by emphasizing the force field each week, we set the expectation that when we engage physically, it's for the purpose of storytelling.

Same deal for "respect the magic sign." For those of you who teach elementary school, it is not unusual to have a class sign that means, "Time to stop what you're doing and pay attention." Our call and response—"Whoop it up?" "Sock it to me!"—has become more than just a way to get the group to pay attention. Sixty percent of the time, it works every time. But it also has become our calling card; when we are in a school building, kids will call out "Whoop it up?", and teaching artists also hear the call out on the streets of Madison. And when we begin a performance, it is a super effective way to get a cafetorium full of kids fired up.

The Man Who Passed Out Who Did Not Go to Jail, Or the Concert That Ended 15 Minutes Early. It is Week 2 of the Whoopensocker residency, and we are writing stories from pictures. I am gathered on the floor with a group of nine kids, a piece of oversized, sticky note paper between us, and we are looking at a picture cut out of a magazine. It is drawn in a Cubist style and depicts a jazz trio. They are likely playing a standing bass, a piano, and a drum set, but the artistic style obscures exactly what instruments they are playing. We "know" it is jazz because the figures are wearing berets and sunglasses, and there are musical notes floating around their heads. We also "know" they are performers because the bottom quarter of the image features cubist versions of the backs of heads sitting in chairs, as if they are an audience watching the three musicians perform.

In group stories, especially in early weeks, the teaching artist does the scribing, while the kids provide the ideas. With a group of eight or more, it is a good idea to both ask for volunteers and call on individual kids who may be less likely to jump into a group brainstorming process. Asks of individual kids can come in the form of specific questions: "Cameron said there were three musicians. What do you want to name them?" Or more general asks: "How should we end this story?" Sometimes, when everyone wants to participate, I go to a round-robin style of participation, where each kid gets a chance to share their idea for the story. The only rule of this process is that you cannot reject anyone's idea (yes, and). You must build on what the person who spoke before you created. Here is what we wrote:

> 3 musicians had been playing jazz for 3 hours on their standing bass and two accordions, when an audience threw an apple at Jerry Curry, and hit him in the head. He passed out, and hit his head on the stage. The other two, Bob and Giannis, were happy, because they secretly wanted him out of the band. Jerry was old, selfish, grumpy, ugly, creepy, and a bad musician. Bob and Giannis did Fortnite dances on his body. First, they clapped. Then, they booed. Then they called the police. After the concert, they arrested everybody, except for Jerry. They just left him there.

The writing flowed pretty well. As you can probably see, I elicited some details—names of the musicians, for example—that likely came from a kid who hadn't yet participated. You can also probably tell that I allowed multiple kids to do some describing: "Old, selfish, grumpy, ugly, creepy, and a bad musician" is a "yes, and . . . " list, if I ever saw one. Not incidentally, when we performed this story, the two people playing Bob and Giannis both referred to Jerry as "old, selfish, grumpy, ugly, creepy, and a bad musician." Keeping this language intact during performance was essential. You can also see that I was asking for an ending and got several. I'm pretty sure when the police arrested everyone, I asked, "but what happened to Jerry?" Their reply—"They just left him there"—is a pretty great answer to that question.

When we got to the title of the story, we had a bit of a tussle. We had one strong vote for "The Man Who Passed Out," which led someone else to say, "The Man Who Did Not Go to Jail," with a late surge for "The Concert That Ended Early." Disagreement bubbled. Sides were taken. And then, I did what Shakespeare did; I offered two titles with an "or" between them to indicate that audiences could take from the story what they chose. *Twelfth Night, or What you Will* is one of my favorite play titles of all time. I love the idea that we as audience members get to decide what to call the play. Thus was born, "The Man Who Passed Out Who Did Not Go to Jail, Or the Concert that Ended 15 Minutes Early." The title itself became part of the experience—when we performed this story for the rest of the class, we made a big deal of the title, enunciating every word and splitting up the line between multiple kids.

Kids often do not get the chance to contribute what they want in a school environment, so when you tell them "every idea is a good idea," it should come as no surprise that they are very interested in pushing the boundaries. Most of what shows up in 3rd grade is stuff like "Fortnite dances" and "Five Nights at Freddy's" and the YouTube sensations of the day. Unless those YouTubers are known racists or criminals, we usually let it slide. We do emphasize that we are interested in new ideas, so if we take an already existing character, we should put them in a new situation. In this story, I'm fairly certain the name Giannis refers to Milwaukee Bucks basketball superstar Giannis Antetokounmpo. Whoever called this name out gets to have their sports fandom valued, while creating an original story mash-up.

Asking our grown-up artists to legitimately learn the floss dance, so they can play Bob and Giannis in a performance of "The Man Who Passed Out . . . " is one of the great joys of my life. There is nothing better than taking a kid's artistic choice seriously, really going for it, and watching their reaction, when they see two "old people" repeatedly floss onstage. And in case you thought I was too highbrow in my humor, I asked our best prat faller, a retired reading teacher in her 60s, to play Jerry. Her entire role in the sketch was to get hit by an apple (carried in slow motion by one of the performers), fall over, and lay there until the end. When everyone had left the stage, she lifted her head and asked, "Where did everybody go?"

Bring the Joy

The most important component of a Whoopensocker performance is celebration. We aim to celebrate the creativity of our authors by recognizing and honoring their contributions to our collective artmaking. Every performance piece begins with a clear statement of the title and author(s) of the story. It is hugely empowering to announce a child's name and story, have them recognize that it is *their* story, and then hear thunderous applause and whoops from their peers and families. Often, that joy is in the form of laughter. We are not above poop jokes.[4] In fact, we love 'em. We are also not above falling down, walking into things, using "the rule of three," or any of the other tropes of comedy that elicit laughs from the young and young at heart. The dumb jokes are the ones that always bring the most joy. In "The Goat on the Tree and the Poor Farmer," our farmer loses his goat (played by a silly human who makes great noises but, otherwise, looks totally human), and can't find her. She is right behind him, trapped in a fake tree. But when he looks everywhere *except* where she is hiding, the kids go nuts. They scream at our hapless farmer, laugh hysterically, and continuously point at goat-woman until eventually he turns around. These 30 seconds spark a lot of joy.

I use the word "joy" and not "hilarity," because joy can also look like celebration. We celebrate individual accomplishments and contributions, especially when we know the writer is not often celebrated for their strengths in the classroom. Teaching artists get to know the kids over the course of our 6 weeks together and so we often select stories from kids who shine in

Whoopers mid-floss, performing "The Man Who Passed Out."

the Whoopensocker context but may struggle in other parts of their school life. We also celebrate how difficult the world can be and how kids navigate those challenges. For example, we took a series of letters that a class wrote during our Make a Change Week in spring 2019 and collected them into a single adaptation. Each of the stories was performed as a series of letters read by different Whoop performers—equally celebrated, equally valued:

Dear Michelle Obama,
Can you please run for president, because the person in the White House is very rude and very mean and very racist. And we need a girl person in the White House. There has never been a girl person in the White House as a president. And, so, your husband has already been president, and it could be a family thing. So, your kids could be a famous person, and they could be a person that is a president. So, next election, please be a person to be elected, because you need to be a person in a famous place, and you would be a more famous person in the White House. So, I hope you like my reason. So, please run for president whenever you want. So, please be president.

Dear Everyone in the World,
We should have more fun at school. We can spend half the day learning and half the day playing. NO MATH! And we should be able to cheat. We can bring our pets and our tablets to school. Teachers only in certain rooms. More ice cream at lunch! And hot chocolate in the winter. We have a right to have fun! Fun is in the needs. Fun can help kids learn better. Kids need fun to create their imagination.

Dear Future Vampire Self,
How is it like being a vampire? Do you have any werewolf friends?

Dear 29-Year-Old Self,
How is your flying unicorn puppy spaceship? If you have one. Have your parents finally agreed to let you be a lawyer's rude person, so you can argue about dogs all day long? I assume you have already adopted 20 dogs, and they have grown wings and started a sweets shop and that you have a cotton-candy hot tub, lollipop, chocolate, and sweet tub.

Dear Donald Trump,
I don't like what you think about the wall because my Grandpa was going to come to visit me but he can't. Can't see my grandpa and grandma. I see the news every day to see if you change. I also pray every day to see if you change but you won't. I want to be the president so I can take down the wall. I know you might be mad if I take down the wall but I want to see my family.

Dear Nothing,
Please become something.

Perhaps my favorite line from any story ever is: "Fun is in the needs." It reminds us that fun, and joy, are not just extras that are nice to have if there's time at the end of the day. In fact, "fun" is a necessary condition for most of Maslow's hierarchy of needs; how can you have your psychological or self-actualization needs met without fun? These are some very wise humans indeed.

ADAPTING STORIES

In Whoopensocker, I am careful not to call us actors, or to refer to our work as "theater." While we do some acting, what we really do is a combination of adaptation and play. That means everything from songwriting to telenovela to choreography to multimedia presentations to short films. Sometimes performance pieces have no words at all. One of our artists loves to create performance pieces entirely with visuals. Through movement, music, and some jokes involving bird-flying contests, she was able to capture the sweetness, humor, and originality of this story entitled "A Bird Adopts a Bird," without ever speaking.

> Once apon a time there was a bird. He was all alone. He wanted company. One day he sea a baby bird. He thoute, "Some compny! I can care for it!" So he went down to it. The baby bird was very welcoming. So he brote it up to his nest. The baby bird grew up to be a very good flyer. He even etered more than 15 flying contests a month! Both of them loved each other a lot. When they got old they enjoyed each others company in a big house they got with all the prize money.
> THE END! (for now!)

In the Whoopensocker show, this piece was performed alongside a fractured fairytale, "Little Red Wolfinghood," which was adapted into a *Hamilton*-style song with full choreography, props, costumes, and choral harmonies. When I first started doing this work, I thought that a focus on artistic diversity was mostly important for the performers. And it is. Everyone gets a chance to flex their artist muscles, and to learn from others how to use muscles they didn't even know they had. Comedians dance during group musical numbers; performers who are just learning Spanish take on speaking roles in Spanish-language stories; younger performers unfamiliar with film noir find themselves playing a Sam Spade–style character in the mystery of who stole the dog food. But artistic diversity is also important for audiences. Live theater "for kids" does not often embrace experimental forms of performance or lean into kids' pop-culture references as mechanisms for sharing stories. We want kids to get comfortable with the idea that a reggae song brings just as much joy as a serious piece about childhood fears. And finally, for the adults in the room, we want them to also enjoy the experience of seeing kids' stories performed in a way that goes beyond the "preciousness" of young peoples' creativity. So, we give them something they can genuinely laugh with, cry with, and, occasionally say, "What the heck was that?!"

The kids' ideas and voices are at the heart of everything we do. If an adaptation has too much joke and not enough story, we abandon it. Sometimes simplest is best—as in the reading of the Make-a-Change letters. In the rehearsal room, we always ask, "What do the kids mean by this?" when interrogating the words and images of their stories. And, if we don't know, we ask the teaching artists. And, if they don't know, we ask the classroom teacher. And then we make adaptation decisions that reflect everyone's collective interpretation of how the kids intended to communicate.

PERFORMING STORIES

Push Boundaries on Norms for Representation

At the same time we aim to represent the kids in our performances, we also want to use performance as a way to invite audiences to question engrained identity norms. Our stories typically contain *a lot* of moms. Makes sense, given that most of our authors are 8 years old. We aim to make as many different choices in the portrayal of "mom" as we have mom characters in our performances. For example, one of our female performers always uses a weightlifting gesture when she comes onstage as a mom; this is instead of wearing an apron and stirring a bowl, a more typical shorthand for "momness." (Of course, if the mom is cooking in the story, then she can be cooking. We don't change content just to change it.) Sometimes male performers will play moms. Without comment and without a wink and a nod to the audience that says, "Yes, we know, this is a man playing a woman. Isn't that ridiculous?" It is simply a man playing a mom. And when we have the opportunity to represent "parents" in a story, we will always choose to have a range of options for what parents can look like—from a single parent to two-parent families with a range of gender combinations.

The Whoopensocker ensemble includes people ages 16–66, and we are careful not to fall into patterns of the youngest ensemble members playing children and the oldest playing adults and people in power. Our performers also come from a variety of backgrounds—some are graduate students, others are professional artists, and some have full-time jobs outside the arts but keep the arts in their lives through their participation in projects like Whoopensocker. We also aim for racial and ethnic diversity that reflects the diversity of the schools, particularly the kids who see predominantly White teachers throughout most of their schooling. This diversity is also important for kids to see what is possible for their future selves. And it is extremely helpful for maintaining a vibrant and constantly changing performance aesthetic.

Honor the Kids' Voices

It is crucial that the performances capture authors' intent. When a group of Whoop artists work on an adaptation, we read the story as we would an August Wilson play. That doesn't mean we can't make changes, or add jokes, but it does mean that we do our best not to alter the tone or message, and we use the kids' words whenever possible.

Honoring the kids' voices also shows up in the way we cast roles within stories. We aim for performers to represent the identity of the writer, especially when the story is about them. Take this example, the text of a Whoopensocker classic, "The Day I Almost Drowned":

> I was 4 years old, and I almost drowned, but let me start from the beginning. I was getting my floatie, when I fell in the water, and I almost drowned, but my stepdad saved me. And I think my stepdad is my hero, and I always stay in the shallow end.

This story was written by an African American, female-identified 3rd grader. The performance features a narrator who tells the story while a performer acts as the child who almost drowned, with the water represented by blue fabric manipulated by two other performers. In a slow-motion, dream-like fashion, the "girl" splashes in the blue fabric, loses a ball, steps and falls onto the fabric, starts to be swallowed up, and is then pulled out by another performer who calms her down, hugs her, and then slowly sends her back out into the calmed water. Whenever we perform this story, the "girl" is always portrayed by an African American female performer to represent the author. The "stepdad" is always played by a male performer, and the narrator's voice is a female voice. Whenever possible, this voice is also an African American performer. Our ensemble aims to have the bodies onstage reflect the bodies in the audience, and not in a tokenized way. It is essential that kids see themselves onstage.

"THE JOE"

That gray day in the middle of March 2019 was a whoopensocker of a day for me. I ran into my favorite kid from the "rambunctious group," as he filed in for the school performance. Let's call him Jack. Jack has, indeed, been rambunctious, hard to keep still, eager to make jokes, and highly pro- lific as a storyteller. I was not involved in the making of the school perfor- mance, so when I showed up that day, I was thrilled to learn that his story, "The Joe," was included in the show. I was even more thrilled to learn that Jack's mom would see the performance. This is possible because we let the classroom teachers know 2 days in advance whose stories we will be performing, so that they can notify caregivers, in case they want to come. I watch Jack see his mom, run over and hug her, and then go and sit on the floor with his friends. I talk briefly to his mom; she tells me that the school principal has sent a cab to pick her up. She is very proud and happy that she is able to see Jack's story performed:

"The Joe"

Once Joe found a dragon. He became friends with the dragon. The dragon was a bad guy, because he breathes fire on people. The people were enraged. They said, "Joe! You better teach that dragon some manners!" He said, "Why? He's not doing anything!" They said, "Yes, he is!" Joe said, "Fine, I'll teach him some manners." He tried to teach the dragon some manners, and the dragon threw a car at him. Joe didn't know the dragon was a shapeshifter. He turned into a human, got into the car, ran into Joe, and, then, went into reverse, and hit him again. Then the ambulance came, and put him in a hospital bed. In the hospital, the people said, "You tried to teach him some manners, didn't you?" "You told me to!" "You did not have to listen." Then everyone got into their car and ran the dragon over.
THE END

After the show, I am full of ideas and excitement, as a researcher and as a teaching artist. I have decided that I will "interview" Jack. We have a quick chat that I record on my phone to capture this moment, so that I can remember how impactful the performance was for him and his family.

Me: Can you tell me what was your favorite thing about working with Whoopensocker?

I am fully expecting him to say, "seeing my story performed," or "having my mom with me when my story was performed." Those of you who are researchers will know that thinking I can anticipate what an interview subject will say in advance is a serious error on my part. If I already know the answer to my question, why am I asking it? Jack does not disappoint.

Jack: My favorite part about Whoopensocker is acting out the stories.

He replies with confidence. I am caught off guard. Though I am off-screen, you can hear the surprise in my voice.

Me: Is what? Was acting out stories? Like, being an actor in the stories?
Jack: Yes.

He says this as if I am the stupidest person in the world for not understanding him the first time. I am not satisfied with this answer, so I keep pressing.

Me: And then how did you feel about seeing your story performed onstage?
Jack: It was funny.
Me: It was funny. Was it what you expected? Or was it different than what you expected?
Jack: It was different; they added a little bit on.
Me: Did you like what they added?
Jack: And they took a little bit away.
Me: Yeah? Can you say a little bit about what was different, and what was the same?
Jack: In my story, it didn't have the tea and the tables. And a dragon threw a car at Joe first.

Scene.

What can we take from this scene? After I scolded myself for thinking I knew Jack better than he knew himself, I felt excited. He took so much from Whoopensocker that seeing his story performed onstage by professional artists in front of his whole school was not even the best part. Also, for Jack, having the chance to get up and *do stuff* in the classroom held a lot of appeal. Performing made him feel good. In terms of his own story, the level of detail that he was able to provide on what was similar and what was different was pretty amazing. This was a story he had written 6 weeks prior to the show and not looked at since. But he remembered that, in his story, the dragon started by throwing a car (as opposed to our version where the car throwing was the culminating event—rule of three, take three actions, and save the most outrageous for last), and he noticed that we added the dragon having tea with Joe as he tried to tame the dragon. His own story had meaning for him, our adaptation had meaning for him, and he was actively able to articulate the differences between the versions. Luckily, I am not on camera during this exchange. I'm pretty sure I cried. I cried teacher tears for all he took from the telling, adapting, and performing cycle and for how just 6 weeks of working in this process showed me what Jack could do.

A quick coda on Jack. He came back to school that night for the evening performance of our show. We offer this second performance so that kids can bring their adults back with them, and we can open the performance up to the greater community. While the school show typically has about 300 kids and 30 adults in attendance, the evening shows have about 50 adults and 50 kids. The vibe is different; we print programs so the adults can see the stories for themselves, and the kids who come get to be super-duper special. Jack walked in, and I went over to say hi—I was very excited to see him back. "Hi, I'm Jack's mom!" said a woman who was not the woman I had met that morning. I shook her hand, told her how much I adored working with Jack, and let them be. Besides, Jack had some other friends at the show, and he wanted to sit up front with them. I was so moved that he felt happy and proud enough to bring all of his moms to the show and that the educators around him—his classroom teachers and the principal—knew that this kind of experience would impact them all. Now, I made *you* cry. We will come back to Whoopensocker throughout our time together. And if you ever get lost in the minutiae of this learning theory or that design principle, you can always return to our motto of why we focus on the arts in our quest to transform teaching and learning: Fun is in the needs.

CHAPTER 2

We Built This City . . .
On Educational Research

Whoopensocker City is built on a strong theoretical foundation of how kids know and learn, with a focus on the assets they bring to the learning environment. A dual focus on individuals and the collective is a hallmark of arts experiences; artmaking works best when we value what each person brings and we work together to create a product or performance that reflects all of our contributions. There is an origin story for this approach that predates Whoopensocker. It begins with the big ideas in education research that have shaped my thinking and form the foundation for an arts-based approach to learning, teaching, and design.

A PLACE FOR COGNITIVE SCIENCE
(AND COGNITIVE SCIENCE IN ITS PLACE)[1]

In the beginning, *cognitive* was defined as knowledge and processes that happen "in the head," meaning how the brain and its component neural systems processed information and created models that represented what was happening in the world. This continues to be an important priority for neuroscience, psychology, and artificial intelligence. As a field, however, cognitive science has moved toward a much richer understanding of knowledge and learning in terms of interactions between minds and worlds—as a cultural, historical and contextual set of processes that is distributed across people, tools, and time (How People Learn II, 2018). So, cognitive science is an important frame, because it acknowledges that understanding what knowledge is and how people get it are crucial questions. But rest assured that these ideas live in a rich tapestry of context, culture, and history.

Constructionism (Constructivism's Newer Model)

Probably one of the most well-known theories across the education enterprise is constructivism. If you are reading this book, you have likely heard the term *constructivism* before, though it is always helpful to read an explanation of a commonly used term multiple times. At its core, constructivism is the idea that all new knowledge is built on already existing knowledge, so that any new thing that you are told, or experience, is filtered through your already-existing knowledge structures. Constructivism was developed in opposition to the previously held "blank slate" model of human cognition, which implied that students were empty vessels just waiting for their head buckets to be filled with the brilliant wisdom of their teachers. The blank slate is a metaphor for human learning that has gone out of fashion, but, in practice, it is still prevalent in many classrooms, from kindergartens through doctoral seminars (Scheurman, 1998).

Constructivism is also closely associated with another popularized phenomenon in education—John Dewey's insight that people learn best by doing (1916). The blank slate metaphor often accompanies a lot of "telling" by teachers, which takes the form of lecture, reading, watching YouTube videos, or, really, any mechanism for communicating information to a passive learner. Since I'm doing a lot of telling, I'll review: the two core tenets of constructivism are:

1. All new knowledge is built on previous knowledge in the form of cognitive, social, cultural, and historical experiences.
2. We learn best by doing something, by putting this new knowledge into use (Steffe & Gale, 1995).

Constructivism helps us understand what learners bring to their learning. Each act of learning is a negotiation between what we already know and the new information we encounter. The concept illustrates how what we bring to learning can overwhelm new lessons so that we turn everything into a version of what we already know. Additionally, it points to how teachers can notice and use the kinds of cultural and historical experiences that learners bring, to shape lessons in ways that draw upon learner resources. Constructivism transforms education from the transmission of knowledge into an interactive communication among teachers, students, families, and communities.

Constructivism has a younger cousin—constructionism. Constructionism with an "n" speaks more directly to the role that cognitive science plays in an arts-based foundation for education. I was doing constructionism *way* before I knew what any of this was. And, if you are a member of my favorite Generation called X, then you have been doing it too. As a Gen Xer, I worked in the programming language LOGO in computer class in middle school. There was an animated turtle on your 8-bit computer screen that you programmed to walk around and create shapes. For example, you could tell your turtle to move 10 paces forward and turn 90 degrees right. You could also tell your turtle to repeat those instructions four times and voila! You could make a square. *That* was the foundation of a constructionist theory of learning, developed by Seymour Papert and first published in the now-classic text, *Mindstorms: Children, Computers, and Powerful Ideas* (1980). Constructionism shifts the metaphor slightly from the constructivist "learning-by-*doing*" to the constructionist, "learning-by-*making*," the literal construction of artifacts that become public displays of knowledge (Papert & Harel, 1991). With this metaphor, learning happens when thinking is worked out through the making of external artifacts. Papert's famous LOGO turtle was first a virtual animal shown on the computer display, then a physical computer-turtle that moved around real-world space, and, finally, with the LEGO/LOGO project, a learner-constructed "turtle" that learners built and controlled via LOGO programming. This progression mirrors the growing theoretical understanding that the more students construct external artifacts, the more they seem to learn.

External Representations

One of the key features of a constructionist theory is the importance of "making things" in both a learning process and as a product of what people learn. Cognitive science developed the idea of mental representations for how a person recreates a model of events or objects in the world. Constructionism builds on this idea with the concept of "external representations." What makes something an external representation? Let's break it down. The *representation* part refers to the creation of a model or an image that highlights certain features of a phenomenon or an experience in order to share a perspective. The *external* part is that the representation actually exists as an artifact in the world outside the mind of its creator. Let me try with my favorite example: a map. What is a map? It is an external representation for helping people navigate the world more easily, given the goals that they have for their navigation. Not all maps are the same, even maps that cover the same territory. A map can be digital or analog, static or interactive. A map for bicyclists will look different from a map for hikers, or a map for drivers. A good external representation, as Don Norman[2] would say, "captures the essential elements of the event, deliberately leaving out the rest" (1993, p. 49). As I often say in classes where I am explaining the power of external representations, "a map of the terrain that *is* the terrain, is not a map."[3] You dig?

Since external representations are super important for knowing, doing, and being, it's not surprising that the capacity to construct them is something we value in our fellow humans. Educational researchers across disciplines have described the capacity to construct an external representation of a complex idea as a marker of mastery (Enyedy, 2005). A representation is an expression of an idea, a feeling, a collaboration, or a reflection on events in a medium that allows you to share with others.[4] Representation occurs when we translate meaning from a thought to a medium, or from one medium to another. The simplest form of representation is the move from thought to speech to conversation. The telling, adapting, and performing process is a series of external representations. When Cameron first wrote the story "When I Broke My Arm," he created an external representation of an event that happened to him and his feelings about that event. When he read it out loud, and Brian and I improvised a performance of that story, we co-created a different external representation. When we brought Cameron's story into the rehearsal room, we offered up a series of external representations that highlighted features of the story that we thought would make the performance dynamic. The decision to anthropomorphize the monkey bars so that we could show the terror Cameron felt at getting back up after falling down created yet another external representation of his story.

Metarepresentational Competence

I want to throw in a fifty-cent phrase here—*metarepresentational competence*—to describe the process of how people learn to construct external representations. Norman emphasizes the importance of creating *metarepresentations*, representations about representations, as the essence of higher-order thought. He says, "It is through metarepresentations that we generate new knowledge, finding consistencies and patterns in the representations that could not readily be noticed in the world" (p. 51). When a kid performs as my mom during True Story Day, they are creating a metarepresentation of my oral retelling of what my mom did, while I was strapped to a hospital bed. Artmaking is guided by the skills of metarepresentation.

What does it look like for people to participate in metarepresentation? Andrea diSessa (2004) describes five tasks that people do with external representations: (1) invent new representations; (2) critique and compare, especially as a way to figure out what representations are good for what goals; (3) understand what representations are for; (4) explain their own and others' representations; and (5) learn new representations without a lot of help. diSessa calls this collection of tasks "metarepresentational competence" (or MRC, for those in the know), and I find that a delightful way to describe the use of representations for learning and demonstrations of learning. diSessa suggests that students possess an innate capacity to develop and display MRC in science, and that these ways of working can provide a link to what scientists do as part of their professional practice. MRC is also present in math classrooms and math learning; Noel Enyedy (2005) demonstrates how kids' invented representations of mathematical concepts is a pathway to developing MRC and to greater success with formalized representations in math. Enyedy shows that kids' understanding of geometric scale through their everyday experiences with blocks and drawing is a useful foundation for developing formalized language of ratios and axes. As metarepresentational competence develops, a learner's ability to represent the desired concepts becomes more understandable to others.

In the arts, MRC means coming to know which artistic tools to use for which communicative purposes. MRC is expressed by making a meaningful connection between the art form and the represented concepts in the process of artmaking. Each art form includes a range of production knowledge, and "moves," that define what it means to know and do. Using ballet as a productive style of dance for expressing the floating nature of hydrogen, and krumping to express the tough, dense nature of iron, is a form of MRC using dance forms and choreography (Solomon et al., in press). Or knowing, as Whoopensocker artists do, that the comedic "rule of three" means that our performance of "The Joe" had to end with a dragon throwing a car, rather than starting with the car-throwing as Jack had originally written it. Arts educators can use MRC as a learning outcome because it is a demonstration of expertise in creating representations through a given art form. Norman calls this, "the essence of intelligence, for if the representation and the processes are just right, then new experiences, insights, and creations can emerge" (1993, p. 47). Agree or not with the whole "essence of intelligence" bit, you have to admit that producing external representations is something we want all learners everywhere to do, and a skill that is trained and refined though artmaking.

Distributed Cognition

Now that we have established the important function that external representations play in knowledge and learning, we should also establish where knowledge and learning live. Constructivism establishes that knowledge builds over time. Constructionism tells us that building is accomplished when people make things and external representations are the result of making things that feature difficult ideas. So, once this happens, where does the knowledge of artmaking reside? How do you find the learning in and through the arts that has happened?

I offer you a relatively simple solution for how to talk about where knowledge and learning live *and* to help understand the role of external representations in sense-making: Pair the word *distributed* with cognition. Distributed cognition emphasizes how the thinking process is "stretched across" actors and external representations in social and cultural situations, as opposed to representations contained in the minds of thinkers. Ed Hutchins's research on ship navigation demonstrated that knowledge of how to pilot a ship is not contained within a single person but rather is stretched across the people and tools in the environment of the ship (1996). The distributed nature of knowledge means we must attend to interactions among participants and the tools that they use as we investigate what those interactions reveal about the social development of knowledge in contexts of action. Distributed cognition shifts the "locus of knowledge" from inside the individual to within and among actor-tool-activity networks (Salomon, 1997).

Distributed cognition fits how artmakers and educators think about learning and assessment. We think of the learning environment as more than just the room where school happens; it's a set of resources for learners that includes artifacts, tools, and people. Ann Brown and her colleagues (1997) describe "communities of learners" as models of distributed expertise where knowledge is co-constructed among the teacher, the students, and the tools that they use, including curricula, technologies, and assessments. In communities of learners, learning and knowledge are situated in interactions among people and tools. No one person owns knowledge, and learning happens as people work together. This model is a useful way to understand the design of learning communities that take seriously the distributed nature of expertise. Distributed cognition is a unifier, not a divider; it describes what knowledge looks like in a constructionist environment (Holbert et al., 2020), while also demonstrating the important role external representations play in teaching and learning (Norman, 1993). Where is the knowledge, for example, of how to tell, adapt, and perform a story? In Whoopensocker, that knowledge is stretched across the teaching artists, the public agreements, the kids' journals, the stories they write (and cowrite), the performance pieces that the artists create, and the performances. Knowledge about Jack's story "The Joe" is stretched across the entire Whoopensocker actor-tool-activity network.

THE NEW LITERACIES

Telling, adapting, and performing stories are acts of literacy. Stories are typically comprised of words, and literacy is commonly understood as comprehending and producing words. Policymakers tend to measure kids' "literacy levels" by efficient measures of vocabulary size and decoding texts through standardized assessments. While Whoopensocker excels at this level of literacy development that is valued by most schools, there is a lot more to the kinds of literacy developed in artmaking than comprehending and producing words. The new literacies gives us a framework for understanding literacy as communication, sophisticated acts of knowing, doing, seeing, valuing, and being. Arts experiences like telling, adapting, and performing stories are perfect manifestations of a richer, more meaningful definition of literacy.

Before we get into the nitty gritty, I want to tell you a story about when my daughter was little. We read tons of books together, but some of my favorites were classic books that I had read as a kid. Among this collection were the Amelia Bedelia books, stories about a hapless but well-intentioned maid who is constantly misinterpreting instructions and, therefore, screwing everything up. "Draw the drapes," her fancy boss lady told her, so Amelia Bedelia presented her with a picture of their drapes. "Dress the chicken for dinner," the fancy lady said. So, Amelia Bedelia put a tiny tuxedo on the evening meal. Amelia Bedelia is a victim of context. She "understands" what her boss is saying from her own perspective, and it's funny because Amelia Bedelia's perspective is not what most adults understand. When I read these stories to my daughter, she did not laugh. And she usually laughed a lot, so this was not a *her* problem. My kid didn't find the stories funny, because she didn't understand the "correct" references. "Draw the drapes" and "dress the chicken" are not phrases that have ever been uttered in my house. She could decode and understand the worlds alright, but she did not understand the frame of reference that made Amelia's responses funny.

From a schooling perspective, it seems sensible to define literacy as decontextualized "reading and writing." After all, the old-school description of what you learn in school—readin', writin', and 'rithmetic—represents two of the essential components. Despite what this aphorism promises, real literacy is *much* more complicated. First of all, what do we mean by "reading" and "writing?" Initially, we meant books. Any "grade-level" appropriate book. By reading, we meant decoding those books, regardless of the interest level of the reader. And by writing, we meant encoding ideas received in school and in forms acceptable to schools. Even if my daughter could have appropriately decoded and encoded Amelia Bedelia, she might have passed the test, but she still did not get the jokes. Something is missing.

The New Literacies helps us move from decoding and encoding to effective communication as the mark of a literate person. I define literacy as producing and consuming ideas using a range of communicative tools to understand and represent complex ideas. This is my definition, but I want to share with you how I have interpreted the work of literacy studies scholars to arrive at this place. Colin Lankshear and Michelle Knobel (2011) provide a groundbreaking framework for understanding what's new in literacy and why this reframing is so important.

1. ***From a psychological to a sociocultural paradigm.*** The psychological metaphor implies that literacy is an individualized act that takes place in the head of the actor, where what it means to "be good" at literacy is fixed and completely external to the task. Our testing regime for literacy is based on a psychological metaphor: "struggling readers" are those who do poorly on external, nonflexible tests of literacy. The "achievement gap" thrives on the identification of struggling readers.
2. ***A discourse theory of literacy.*** The shift to a sociocultural metaphor requires that we bring in the concept of *discourse* as a way to explain the role of context in literacy. The sociocultural paradigm for literacy positions "discourse" as literacy, where "being good"

at literacy is situated within the ways of knowing, doing, seeing, valuing, and believing that are part of that discourse community. According to Jim Gee (1989), we all have a primary discourse based on the community we are raised in, and a series of secondary discourses that we acquire by engaging in different communities of practice over time. School is a secondary discourse, one that everyone must learn to be a part of over time. As with all things, this learning is made easier for some people than others, as the ways of knowing, doing, seeing, valuing, and believing that comprise school are closer to some primary discourses than to others. So, a sociocultural paradigm allows us to acknowledge the political component of literacy: Some peoples' discourses are more closely aligned to school contexts for "what counts" as literacy (Gee, 1989). In Whoopensocker, when we focus on kids' ideas and not on their spelling, we are bridging the contexts of literacy that matter in the everyday lives of learners into the school world. It is *much* more important that they write letters to Michelle Obama and their future vampire selves than it is that they put a period in the right place. The confidence to make an argument, in writing, that you can run for president in order to "take down the wall," that's the real stuff. The grammar we can fix.

3. **Literacy is displayed across media forms.** The New London Group (1996) first argued that our conceptions of literacy should be expanded to include multiple modalities for communication. The digital-media arts include not only reading and writing but many other media for communication, including still and moving images, sound, and music. The increased accessibility of simple digital-media tools has accelerated this shift to multimodal literacies.

   Knobel and Lankshear summarize literacies as "reading, writing, and comprehending [involving] combinations of text, still and moving images, sound, and so on" (2017, p. 217). If you're old enough, you may have played the game *SimCity* on your PC. If you haven't kept up, *SimCity* has turned into playing *The Sims* on any digital device—computer, tablet, phone, whatever you've got. But playing the Sims has become more than just playing the game itself. Playing also means accessing "mods," online through user communities that allow the player to customize the game. These mods are fan-created and players share and access this content through user-curated websites. Anyone can create mods; anyone can use each other's mods. Players watch YouTube videos of other people playing *The Sims*, which get millions of views. Some of these YouTubers earn their living playing the Sims and having folks watch them. Players watch these videos, comment on them in YouTube chats, and even take some of these conversations "offline" by messaging with other commenters through Instagram where they post snapshots of their Sims characters in their Sims world. The Sims is not some crazy aberration—more and more, literacy expertise in the everyday world is marked by participation in a variety of media forms stretched across virtual and in-person worlds. New *media* literacies describes how this shift in modes and forms greatly expands the traditional meaning of literacy as decoding and encoding text.

4. *Literacy (and grammar) develop in real time.* Young people today are producing and consuming more text than any other generation. From a traditional literacy perspective, the practices of texting and YouTube can look like efforts to undermine academic English usage. However, ways of expressing ourselves have always evolved over time, and schools need to respond to the rapidly evolving means of consuming and producing text and images as expansions of the canon. As the walking tube of lipstick in the Whoopensocker classic story "Butt stick" said, as she looked at herself in the mirror, "LOLOLOLOL." Text language like "LOL" is now regularly used in everyday discourse. All written language, when new, is controversial, and takes some time to become accepted as a standard. At one time it was Shakespeare, and now it is hip-hop. Accepting that language (and modalities for communication and expression) change is part of a new literacies perspective.

Multiliteracies

New literacies' relative, multiliteracies, deserves a mention here. The New London Group (1996) coined the term in response to the reframing I just described. The "multi" part refers to both the modes available for meaning-making and the forms of communication beyond printed text that represent a single cultural perspective. Multiliteracies is built on the idea that knowledge is embedded in social, historical, cultural, and physical context, and that learning happens at the intersection of these, primarily through the design and sharing of representations. NLG member Brian Street provides this great summary:

> Rather than a single literacy with a uniform set of basic or technical skills, literacies include multicultural uses of texts to get things done in everyday life. Every site of learning, whether in school or out of school, is a unique cultural context with particular social practices (including literacies) that are valued among people. (2017, p. 505)

An important feature of the multiliteracies perspective is an emphasis on literacy as a *social practice*, meaning something that is enacted among

people in a particular place. This is consistent with the sociocultural paradigm shift of the new literacies. What's extra here is that scholars talk about
literacy as an act of *design*—that doing literacy involves a variety of design
practices. That can mean anything from crafting sentences and gestures to
ordering our morning coffee to producing a representation of ourselves with
a 3D printer. If literacy is an act of design, then we are necessarily designing
for, meaning literacy involves an audience as one way to understand social
practice (Cope & Kalantzis, 2000). This model of multiliteracies fits perfectly into the model of artmaking as knowing and doing. So, multiliteracies is a
lot like new literacies, but with an emphasis on design, or making, as a core
part of what it means to "do" literacy.

Critical Literacies

Okay, one more related term. Critical Literacy is the New Literacies' political relative, the one who rolls up to holiday dinners on her motorcycle and
tells the kids about what life is like on the open road. We can't leave her
out of the dinner-table conversation. Critical literacies emphasize the power
relationships embedded in all acts of literacy—"Critical literacy is thus a political project that seeks to build an activist citizenry that fights for equity"
(Larson, 2017, p. 164). Educator and philosopher Paulo Freire is recognized
as a founder of modern critical education. He emphasizes the crucial role of
literacy in raising consciousness, what he calls "reading the word and the
world" (Freire & Macedo, 1987). Critical literacy serves as a mechanism
for social justice that works alongside oppressed peoples rather than doing
something to or for them. Most of what happens in Whoopensocker and in
arts practices everywhere are acts of critical literacy, as we use stories and
performances as vehicles for empowering kids' points of view.
    The critical frame intersects directly with how we've already been
talking about literacy in three ways: first, critical literacies focuses on the
perspectives from which texts, books, movies, podcasts are presented, and
how producers and consumers act in relationship to these perspectives.
How are young people with autism, for example, positioned in different
genres of text? *The Curious Incident of the Dog in the Night-Time* (novel
by Mark Haddon, play by Simon Stephens) is a mystery story told from the
perspective of a 15-year-old with autism. It is not, however, a book *about*
autism, creating opportunities for a range of relationships between the producers and consumers of these media texts.
    Second, critical literacies values multimodality (the use of multiple
modes of expression both individually and in combination) as methods of
expression. This is, in large part, because new multimodal combinations
often emerge from the innovative practices of historically disenfranchised
communities. Take printmaking as an example. Printmaking is both an art
form and an act of protest and resistance. The Chicano Art Movement iden-

tifies printmaking as a core practice that involves Mexican and American visual art tools and techniques that are often directed toward political action through the public display of protest images. This is evident in the Smithsonian exhibit ¡Printing the Revolution!, which covers the history of "Chicano" art from 1965 to the present, highlighting the role of images, text, and icons in meaning-making (https://www.artandobject.com/press-release/printing-revolution-rise-and-impact-chicano-graphics). As a multimodal form, a print, typically, involves images, text, and color that are collectively designed to express a message toward change.

A critical literacies perspective takes a social-justice approach to teaching and learning through social action (Morrell, 2008). It seeks to change the way learners act in the world by empowering them to become part of a culture of power. Whoopensocker's "make a change" day seeks to do just this. Kids express joy: "More ice cream at lunch!" They express transgressive opinions about our political leaders: "I also pray every day to see if you change but you won't." And they imagine futures: "How is your flying unicorn puppy spaceship?" As literacy scholar Donna Alvermann says, "the pursuit of social justice is a mainstay of the critical literacies framework" (2017, p. 474).

CULTURALLY RELEVANT AND SUSTAINING PEDAGOGIES

A constructionist, new-literacies frame for understanding teaching and learning requires that educators take seriously what kids know and can do, and that we honor their contributions to our learning environments as unique and necessary for successful, collective outcomes. This is what we do in Whoopensocker, and this is how we can begin to change our approach to how teachers and schools work with kids on a broad scale. As it currently stands, educators' jobs are often framed as "fixing broken kids," and measuring how well we've fixed them by how much they improve on the tests that we've developed to demonstrate their worth. This is deficit thinking; even the language of "intervention" as a method of improving what's not working for kids in classrooms implies that something has gone terribly wrong, like in a disaster movie. Ugh. Asset-based pedagogies provide an antidote for the deficit-thinking poison. To put us all on the same page,[5] asset pedagogies refers to a fundamental, constructivist shift in the way we understand what all communities bring to teaching and learning. In their field-defining volume, *Culturally Sustaining Pedagogies*, Paris and Alim describe the shift as

> Reposition[ing] the linguistic, literate, and cultural practices of working-class communities—specifically, poor communities of color—as resources and assets to honor, explore, and extend in accessing White middle-class dominant cultural norms of acting and being that are demanded in schools. (2017, p. 4)

This is an important point that cannot be overstated. If we begin our work as educators, designers, researchers, parents, and students with the idea that the function of schooling is to *make up for what kids lack*, we are always going to be framing some kids as less than others. Asset pedagogies fundamentally change the conversation by requiring that we attend to what communities bring to teaching and learning and to have those assets serve as the foundation of our work. Does that mean that schools have nothing new to teach? Of course not—that's why we have schools. But does it mean that a full remaking of our sense of who brings what value to the classroom is required? Yup, that too.

Culturally Relevant Pedagogy and Teaching

I have been lucky enough to work at the University of Wisconsin–Madison with Dr. Gloria Ladson-Billings as my colleague. She is one of the most famous education researchers in the world, in no small part because of her pioneering work defining culturally relevant pedagogy (CRP) and putting young peoples' assets at the center of conversations about how to do teaching better. Folks call Gloria the OG; she published the article on CRP that earned her that honor in 1995, and followed up with the shift to culturally sustaining pedagogy in 2014. As Paris and Alim (2017) describe, CRP has become a near-ubiquitous term in the preparation of teachers, professional development programs, and policy conversations that focus on the experiences of Black and Brown children. Of this fundamental change, Gloria says, "Instead of asking what was wrong with African American learners, I dared to ask what was right with these students and what happened in the classrooms of teachers who seemed to experience pedagogical success with them" (2014, p. 74). CRP offers us a lens for how asset pedagogies can look in the classroom, specifically, how educators can choose to focus on the kinds of content and process that will connect to kids' personal and cultural lives. CRP gives us permission to acknowledge kids' cultural lives as a key component of what a successful teaching space should look like. The idea that we ought to celebrate what kids bring to their learning (rather than encourage kids to come in as blank slates) may seem obvious now. If it does, that's due, in large part, to Gloria's work.

In her more recent writings, the OG of CRP has turned her head toward the framing of culturally sustaining pedagogy, a "remixed" version that takes a fluid perspective on culture. Gloria's work still centers the relationship between learning and an understanding and appreciation for students' cultural knowledge and positioning. It also asks us to examine "culture" as hybrid, dynamic, and complex. She embraces hip-hop as a paradigmatic example of a culturally sustaining practice, which has natural connections to the arts as a way of knowing, doing, and being.

Culturally Sustaining Pedagogy

Culturally sustaining pedagogy (CSP) as a "remix" is a useful framing for work that features the role of the arts in teaching, learning, and design. CSP maintains the asset-based perspective that Gloria so successfully introduced into the discourse and moves beyond justifying the inclusion of cultural practices of youth communities of color in schooling to ask, "For what purposes and with what outcomes?" (Paris & Alim, 2017, p. 5). This remix-as-metaphor is itself artistic: While you can remix anything, we popularly think about a "remix" as taking already existing media (songs, poems, videos) and putting them together in novel ways. Constructionism also includes "remixing" as a practice of taking preexisting ideas and creating novel representations (Wilkerson & Gravel, 2020).

The scholars who are at the center of the CSP movement have brought hip-hop forward as an artistic, social, literary, and linguistics youth movement that has defined the past 50 years in global culture (Wong & Alim, 2017). In her contribution to the CSP volume, Gloria describes her own transformation in terms of a realization that she was missing attention to *youth* culture, most notably how young peoples' identity expressions manifest in "their dress, their language, their dance, their art, their fascination, and facility with technology, and above all their music" (Ladson-Billings, 2017, p. 147). Hip-hop as an art form provides a core set of practices for the CSP classroom. Casey Wong and Courtney Peña assert that the arts function as culturally sustaining practices by leveraging students' interests in the arts, which they note, "were helping [young people] survive their day-to-day lives and, beyond that, uplifting their communities" (2017, p. 120). As they describe, the arts offer possibilities for joy, while also making space for the kinds of culturally sustaining experiences that represent young peoples' lived realities that are often difficult and deemed inappropriate for school. Both culturally relevant pedagogy—and the culturally sustaining remix—are the strongest foundation I know for framing our understanding of what good teaching, learning, and design ought to be *and* how they connect naturally to the arts.

Cultural Modeling

I want to call out to a theoretical strand of this work that has had a huge influence on me and has particular traction for understanding how the arts intersect with culturally sustaining pedagogies. The great Dr. Carol Lee developed the cultural-modeling framework (Lee, 2001) and realized the power of this framework in classrooms (Lee, 1995). As a former English teacher and cofounder of an African-centered school in Chicago (www.bsics.org), Carol focused her ideas on connecting students' cultural funds of knowledge with school-based content, especially response to literature. Cultural modeling is about identifying the assets students bring to the language-arts classroom and leveraging those assets as scaffolding for interpreting and understanding canonical literature—everything from Toni Morrison to Shakespeare.

I had the opportunity to work directly with Carol on a project that centered the role of African American discourse features in younger children's creative practices. In the Cultural Modeling and Narrative project, the team created a curricular project for a group of elementary school children from an all–African American school who had been identified as "struggling readers and writers." The project involved selecting what Carol calls a "cultural data set" of paintings by Annie Lee[6] to serve as a scaffold between kids' experiences and school-sanctioned practices, like drawing and writing stories from pictures. In our analysis of how kids responded to these pictures through oral and written language, we found that kids' use of African American discourse features[7] was not only prevalent throughout their storytelling but that the quality of their storytelling was vastly improved when they used familiar cultural assets (Lee et al., 2004). This work has been the foundation of the role of images in our Whoopensocker classrooms; we dedicate a whole week to writing stories from images, and we are purposeful in our selection of images that will engage kids' cultural funds of knowledge. Cultural modeling also offers a direct link between the CSP movement, literacy studies, and the arts as the foundation for teaching, learning, and design.

BRINGING COGNITIVE SCIENCE, THE NEW LITERACIES, AND ASSET PEDAGOGIES TOGETHER THROUGH THE ARTS

The Whoopensocker process is a great illustration of how these big ideas come together into real life practices of teaching and learning. The writing, adapting, and performing of "The Man Who Passed Out . . ." is a series of external representations that begins with a cubist drawing and ends with grown people flossing and calling their bandmate, "old, selfish, grumpy, ugly, creepy, and a bad musician." All of these representations are themselves literacy practices; we wrote together, we performed what we wrote for the whole class, and the Whoopensocker team created a version of the story that elevated the original writing to a professional performance. The original story is comprised entirely of kids' contributions, highlighting their social and cultural resources. Cognitive science and the new literacies come together around making things as the central focus of teaching and learning, and a critical perspective is a crucial component of all making-as-learning activities.

The Importance of Making Things

Constructionism introduces learning *by* making; the social context shapes students' learning and serves as a repository from which learners can draw resources to work out their thinking using more concrete methods. Meanwhile, the new literacies describe learning *in* making and positions the context of constructing as the place in which learning happens. Both center design where learners weave together multiple tools and modes for meaning-making as they create representations. The process and practice of making *and* the participation in community equally define making. For example, Barajás-Lopez and Bang's (2018) Claywork project brings an Indigenous knowledge perspective to understanding learning through making with Native youth. They center Indigenous artmaking practices—claymaking and weaving—as mechanisms for learning about ecosystems. Of particular note is their simultaneous focus on the necessity of both the making process (valued in constructionism) and the sharing process (valued in multiliteracies), in identifying underlying issues of culture, power, and knowledge in the learning process.

Whoopensocker is all about making things; kids write and perform as constructionist acts of literacy that start with what kids bring to the table. Just like the Claywork project, we focus on both making and sharing as methods of including the practices, values, and ideas that matter to our young authors and to our teaching artists.

Criticality Is Critical

One other connection that may be obvious to you, but we should make sure to say out loud—the word "critical" is crucial to all of these concepts. "Critical" implies attention to the role of power, inequality, and marginalization in discussions of teaching and learning. We saw pretty clearly how the new literacies have a strong critical focus (heck, there's a whole subfield that calls itself "critical literacies"). And Freire's ideas have been used to better understand constructionist learning environments: Making, tinkering, and crafting could all be considered acts of radical, critical production. Good troublemaker Paulo Blikstein (2020) has been banging this gong for a while; his new essay, "Cheesemaking Emancipation," articulates a theory of critical and cultural making that goes beyond romanticizing "working with your hands" to a truly emancipatory approach that, "take[s] students from the acceptance of one's given reality to the possibility of changing it" (p. 123).

Critical perspectives are also in direct conversation with culturally relevant and sustaining pedagogies. Bringing youth and community cultural assets into the classroom is itself a critical act; daring to position what young people know as not only valuable but crucial to what happens in schools is a direct challenge to traditional power relationships and to canonical knowledge. The OG herself has written about the twin topics of culturally relevant pedagogy and critical race theory (Ladson-Billings & Tate, 1995)—they are mutually informing ideas that center issues of power and inequity in our work to make positive changes to teaching and learning. In Whoopensocker, we aim for a critical perspective in writing—it's OK to write about what's wrong and what's right with the people in power around us—and in performance—we purposefully show multiple perspectives on the same idea, like what it means to be a parent or a family. A letter to the President about taking down the wall performed word-for-word alongside a goodnight lullabye where single, same sex, and differently sexed parents get equal stage time lives comfortably in the land of critical perspectives.

So, now you know my best shot at explaining the three big ideas that have shaped the way I understand teaching and learning. These are not the only ideas in education, but they are the ones that help me to explain why the arts are so powerful and the ways that we can transform our teaching and learning settings to take advantage of what the arts have to offer. You might be thinking, "What do I need the rest of this book for? She's already given us the tools that we need to be successful!" I wouldn't blame you for thinking that. But hold on, because where the magic happens is how these ideas come together in the arts.

CHAPTER 3

Learning in and Through the Arts

At Whoopensocker, our lead teaching artists create reflection journals as a way to keep records of our time in schools and to highlight practices that work, and don't work, with students. Several years ago, I followed a student, whom I call Nick, throughout our residency.

> Week 1: Nick was super excited to come up with the group story and participate in all aspects of the performance. He was such a strong contributor in the group that Janine had to tell him to hold off a few times. Meanwhile, in individual writing time, he jumped right into writing. His writing is enthusiastic and clear, though he really struggles with the technical aspects of writing (grammar, spelling, fine motor skills). It does not seem to stop him from participating in any way.

At this point, I knew *nothing* about Nick. I chose to write about him in my reflection because he stood out to me as an enthusiastic participant and performer on day one. One of those kids that we would refer to as a star, which, in my experience, means his teacher and school would not describe him that way. I've been in this game long enough to spot a kid like that. Nick's story can help us to reimagine how we ought to support and measure learning in schools through the arts.

AN ARGUMENT IN FAVOR OF TRANSFORMING LEARNING

Learning is a natural process that everyone does all the time. However, over the years, our schools have adopted a model of learning that seems anything but natural and far from how learning happens in the arts. As arts educators, we consistently face a mismatch between how and what people learn in the arts and what counts as learning in schools. School-based learning tends to assume that the outcomes for learning are fixed—a set of math skills, a body of social studies content, new verb conjugations in language class. In the arts, learning outcomes are emergent and collective; we expect students to bring their histories and experiences with them to come together to create something original. Thinking of learning as novel, emergent, and collective can be a huge transformation of how we see education. And we can't legitimately change the way we teach if we don't transform what learning looks like. That starts with changing our values around what counts as good learning.

For a long time in formal education, we have placed our highest values on outcomes we can measure so that results can be compared across learners. But learning is not what is captured in the results—it is a process that precedes the measurement. Many of my colleagues who study learning fail to question the underlying assumptions that lead them to value reading scores or interest in STEM careers as the proxies for successful learning. As I write this, there is a movement stirring to reject these proxies for what counts as good learning at scale. My kid is a freshman in high school, and, by the time she applies to college, the ACT and SAT will likely no longer be required for college admissions. Gloria Ladson-Billings has called for a "hard reset" on education and for us to fundamentally reconsider the kind of human beings we want to produce (2021). What we test reflects what we value and support; and what we ignore gets set aside as extra (and irrelevant) for learning. Gloria focuses on the features of culturally sustaining pedagogy as core commitments for the reset; arts practices can, and should, also be at the center.

One of the main reasons for a reset is that school practices regularly devalue the kinds of knowledge, skills, and identities that people bring from their lives outside of school. To illustrate, let me return to Nick's experience in Whoopensocker, in Week 5, Make a Change:

> Nick worked with his aide on an argument—"I believe dreams are important." He doesn't write at all, but he has tons of creative ideas, and he really thinks beyond the parameters of the writing prompt. He understood the task and was eager to express his ideas about dreams. Figuring out how to translate those to paper is a daunting task, but it feels good that he is able to focus enough to build the argument alongside an adult.

At the time, I certainly didn't remember what I'd written 4 weeks earlier about Nick and his enthusiastic participation. You can see here that I position Nick as a collaborative creator (working with his aide in Week 4), rather than focusing on his individual contributions (jumping right into writing in Week 1). But this collaborative work does not make the ideas any less his or take away from his learning about arguments and how to make them. Intrigued by Nick's continued participation and success, I followed him into Week 6:

> Nick and Gustavo both took lead roles in my performance. Nick played a unicorn (a superhero unicorn—this part was his invention) and Gustavo

played the evil queen with the giant turtle. Also, I sat with Nick during some of the other performances. When it came to a story from our class, he said, "I seen this one before!" Amazing how much he remembered from Weeks 1 and 2 and how the ideas were familiar, even though it seems like there's chaos when we're performing.

Nick was one of my favorite kids in this residency. Sitting side by side and talking during a performance is my marker that someone thinks enough of me to share that experience. It felt special. Nick was also super proud of the unicorn horn he made for his performance. He insisted we use props and costumes and innovated the use of string to tie around his head. Several other unicorns followed suit.

> Post-program reflection: I had a conversation with Ms. M [Nick's aide] about Nick and Gustavo. When I told her how great they both were, she told me they are both "highly autistic" and have a hard time participating in group work. She said, "Nick never does anything," and that she's been sending pictures of him participating in Whoop to his mom! She talked about how great it is to see Nick being successful and to see his imagination come through, his ability to work in a group, and to stay focused on a task.

The only reason I have this photo of Nick, Gustavo, and I performing together is because a teacher thought it was important enough to capture, and send along to the kids' moms. This moment represented a powerful example of learning that she could share with parents who persistently get the message that their kids aren't good enough, and that typically they fail to learn what the other children learn.

HOW CAN THE ARTS RESHAPE LEARNING?

How can we use the arts to explain what Nick was learning? How can we give voice to a new system of values around what we ought to learn? Now that we know the theories of learning that help us understand why the arts matter, we can build on these principles to develop new approaches to teaching and schooling. I want to ask not what learning can do for the arts—but what the arts can do for learning. I propose a new system of learning principles, tied to participation in arts practices:

1. People who make art learn to *create, share and critique representations*, which is the foundational process for being a successful student.

Nick, Gustavo, and I perform in the group story, "Infection 2: Dancing Unicorns and the Fortnight Death Scene"

2. Artmaking flows from and develops *identity* as a process of
   experimenting with and becoming and as a product of creating,
   doing, and enacting;
3. In the arts, *collaboration* is an outcome. People learn to collaborate
   through participating in arts practices.

The arts make these outcomes possible in ways that help schools develop more robust and engaging learning environments. It is our job to invest in making sure these principles are valued and achieved.

Creating, Sharing, and Critiquing Representations

While all school-based disciplines value external representations (e.g., homework), the arts are especially well-suited to understanding how creating and sharing representations is at the core of good learning. Philosopher Nelson Goodman is one of my faves in thinking about creating representations through art. As founding director of Harvard's Project Zero,[1] he set up the conditions for us to think about artmaking as fundamentally an act of representation. In his 1976 book about the philosophy of art, he describes the different forms of representation as "referring to" ideas, concepts, or objects in the world. Representations in art are filled with form and meaning, and these are often inseparable. What artmakers mean is carried by their work as a medium of communication to an audience. Art representations evolve with changes in arts practices, tools, and media—both for individual art makers and for artmaking communities over time.

Representations have both transient and durable qualities. More permanent media, such as pictures, photos, text, or video, can be enjoyed in shows and exhibitions, or in conversations, or at concerts. Whoopensocker performances are representations that happen at a certain time and place but can be referred to by sharing a score, script, or recording of the performance. Every time you translate an idea to a new medium, you make a new representation. Art thrives in this process of re-presenting ideas and inspiration across media to new audiences. In each artmaking process, a new set of representations draws upon a set of knowledge and skills that is built over time that guides the artist to use media and tools in new ways. Making successive representations deepens technical knowledge and communicates new ideas to a wider range of audiences.

Representations include two components: ideas and media. Artmaking is creating a fit between these two so that the idea can come across and be communicated through the media. Eliot Eisner, arts education's most eloquent and passionate leader, articulates for us how the core of arts practice involves understanding the relationship between materials and how they express an idea. "Getting smart," Eisner wrote about art in school, "means coming to know the potential of the materials in relation to the aims of a project or problem; and since each material possesses unique qualities, each material requires the development of distinctive sensibilities and technical skills" (2002). Selecting the right media and knowing how it can be manipulated for successful communication, is an important feature of the artmaking process.

Both Goodman and Eisner are pointing to the same core insight: Producing art is a communicative act that requires learners to master the representational tools of the artistic medium. Tools for representation vary with the forms of art themselves; dance requires bodies and choreography, digital media requires multimodal tools, and the visual arts require everything from paint brushes to clay. To use tools effectively, artists have to understand how they support communication within a specific context and what is possible within a given art form. It is not enough to know how to use an audio-editing tool like GarageBand; artmakers must understand what forms of audio editing are expected and acceptable within a specific art form, for example, to produce a documentary radio piece.

What Does It Look Like for Artmakers to Participate in Representation? The musical *Spring Awakening* (2006) is an adaptation of a German play written in the 1890s, with music by pop star Duncan Sheik and choreography by Bill T. Jones, that makes teen angst uniquely accessible to audiences. From a learning perspective, the dance form representation carries the audience from the core idea (teen angst) through the tools of representational medium (choreography by Jones). Each form of arts technique is composed of tools. The "tools" are the artifacts, either conceptual or physical, that describe the "moves" artmakers can use to create art in a given medium. In dance, the tools include physical artifacts such as shoes, floors, costumes, and props. But they also include conceptual artifacts that describe the catalogue of movement in that genre of performance—such as ballet or krumping—and how those movements interact with music. Choreographers use the tools of dance to organize performers for expression.

Beginning artmakers become acquainted with the tools of their art form by interacting in communities already familiar with the tools. As artmakers become more proficient, they begin to use tools to express the typical or classical representations in the media, then, with increasing mastery, move on toward the representation of new ideas. As an expert choreographer, Jones developed new kinds of tools (combinations of moves, sequences, and relationship to music) that express new understandings. We can talk about these tools broadly—how musicals have songs, dances, and scripts—and on a micro level—what certain styles of dance might allow you to communicate. Across art forms, artmakers use organizing tools to compose the overall features of a piece or a performance, and use microlevel tools to etch out each particular aspect of the expression.

The process where artmakers come to learn the relationship between ideas and tools is what I call the *representational trajectory* (Halverson, 2013). As artmakers progress in their work, they create a series of representations including outlines, rough cuts, sketches, notes, and thumbnails that demonstrate the evolution of their expressions. A learner's representational trajectory charts a path from initial conception to final piece through successive representations. Each representation displays an emerging understanding of how the artmaker uses (or does not use) the available tools. Documenting this trajectory provides opportunities for educators to assess progress and to deliver "just-in-time" guidance about next steps. In creating representations, artists come to understand the relationship between concepts and tools, as well as between their individual work and the broader arts community.

Many new artmakers do not know how to use an unfamiliar medium, and struggle with how to express their ideas. The representational trajectory demonstrates how emerging artists move toward more expert practice. It includes two tracks for the development of learning: a narrative track for the development of the idea, and a technical track to document tool-learning. Figure 3.1 represents a typical representational trajectory in artmaking: For many artmakers, the process starts with a focus on the story (what they want to communicate), moves to a focus on how the tools of the artistic medium affords multiple representations of these ideas, and ends with a consideration of the relationship between these two aspects of artmaking. Tracing this trajectory through multiple representations provides a powerful tool to assess the progress of artmakers.

The representational trajectory documents artmaking as learning from initial idea to final performance or sharing. Take the piece created by 16-year-old digital artist Frank at Street Level Youth Media in Chicago in 2007. He participated in a summer program called Represent! Exploring Your Identity Through History and Culture. Frank made an autobiographical graphic-design piece made up of three elements: (1) a photoshopped image of himself superimposed in front of two flags; (2) a black- and-white line drawing of a person split down the middle; (3) a series of names/nicknames printed on individual placards placed below the images. The representational trajectory of his artmaking can be traced by examining the development of ideas through his journal, interviews, and final piece.

Frank created a series of representations, including brainstormed lists of names that people call him, photographs that he took with his mentor, and sketches of potential layouts. Some of these initial ideas were carried over into the final piece—he sketched a series of representations of "border crossing from Mexico to USA"—while others were dropped. The largest image in Frank's final piece is a screen-printed color image of him and two simplified flags, Mexican and American. In interviews conducted mid-process, Frank attributed the idea of border crossing to his father who brainstormed ideas about identity with him that focused on "doing something about being Mexican and American." Frank also described how his artist-mentor inspired him to make the flags more of his own. By combining his love for

Figure 3.1. The representational trajectory in artistic production processes

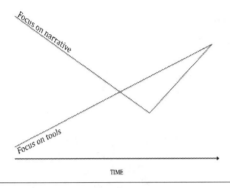

Focus on narrative

Focus on tools

TIME

Source: Halverson, E. (2013). Digital art making as a representational process. *Journal of the Learning Sciences*, 22(1), 121–162. Reprinted by permission of the publisher (Taylor & Francis Ltd, http://www.tandfonline.com).

the alternative, industrial rock band Nine Inch Nails and his commitment to his Mexican/American border crossing identity, Frank created simplified, but recognizable, flags in the style of one of their album covers. Frank's mentor moved him from initial idea to a set of practical graphic design–style representational tools that he could use to demonstrate Frank's core idea of border crossing.

Frank's compelling final representation allowed him to share the story of his identity through new media. The artist statement he wrote to accompany his public art work explains the apex of his trajectory: "This is a graphic design piece dealing with being a Mexican American, crossing borders each day going to different places with his art work and gathering all of his names." Using the representational trajectory allows us to see how Frank's understanding of his idea and his mastery of the art form progressed. Through multiple iterations of this representation, he was able to create and share himself using forms that no one had used before. He was also able to articulate why he chose the tools he did, who helped him, and how the forms in his piece communicate meaning. Tracing Frank's representational trajectory allows us to see into his artmaking as a learning process.

Critique and the Representational Trajectory. Critique is an important language practice to advance the ideas and the media development of the representational trajectory. Critique is the careful practice of looking at other peoples' representations and offering responses that can help them see what you see. A good critique ought to ask people to stop, reflect, and articulate how well the artistic process represents the ideas the artist is trying to communicate. Critique calls for a particular kind of language practice that arises when groups of artists are sharing works in progress with one another and seeking feedback.

Critique happens in episodes, when young artists articulate how they interpret choices being made, what they think external audiences will understand about these choices, and how the creator might take this feedback forward into future iterations of their work. The stages of a representational trajectory inform which kind of critique is most helpful at which stage of the artmaking process. In the beginning stages, critique can be helpful to clarify ideas and to guide new artmakers toward the basic tools necessary for initial representations. Midway through the process, critique can begin to focus on the appropriate use of the tools, and suggestions about techniques that could advance or complement the emerging representations. Near the end of the artmaking, critique can inform the fit between the idea and the tools in order to refine the representation, and could even support the transition to a new artmaking project using ideas inspired by the initial process.

Lissa Soep's work with young people making movies and radio stories has documented many such episodes of critique, which she characterizes as opportunities for developing and applying judgment, using the specific language of the artistic medium. "Their mastery of vocabulary, such as wide shots and medium shots," she says of teens working together to produce a narrative film about tensions between two generations of Asian American youth, "allowed them to speak in a kind of shorthand through which they could express, evaluate, and finally execute the scene" (Soep, 2006, p. 762). Critique is inherent to arts practice because it is a core component of the representational trajectory.

Language Learning Through Representation. One of my sheroes, world-famous linguistic anthropologist Shirley Brice Heath, studied arts organizations as productive sites for language learning and use (Heath, 2000). She found that being in a situation where artmaking is happening, like a theater club, an out-of-school visual-arts program, or a dance team, led young people to be more flexible in their use of language and better able to adapt to the range of situations where they would have to communicate. If you want to communicate with a gallery owner about how to present your painting, you have to be clear about how the space where it's hanging interacts with your artwork. If you are the ticket taker, you have to communicate with all kinds of patrons who have a range of experiences seeing live theater. And when you mentor new members, you have to use both the language of the organization and the language of those who may talk and think the way you did when you started out several years earlier.

In arts practices, language is learned through the acquisition and use of artistic forms. Language learning means generating representations in terms of communally accepted norms to effectively communicate with an audience. The narrative arts (theater, filmmaking, spoken-word poetry, podcasting, etc.) are linked most directly to the development of language. Group composition, journal writing, story pitches, scriptwriting, editing, and re-mixing are all typical activities in narrative artmaking that center language learning and language use as part of the representational trajectory (Halverson & Gibbons, 2010). In theater programs where young people create original, live performance pieces based on their own stories, wrestling with meaning through language is an ongoing process (Halverson, 2007; Wiley & Feiner, 2001). Young people must constantly make a range of linguistic decisions, as they first tell stories out loud, then transition to printed scripts that can be used for rehearsal and performance (Halverson, 2010b). Should a new character be included to represent a certain aspect of the narrative? Should the specifics of an individual person's story be sacrificed to make a broader cultural point through the combination of multiple languages, or through changes to one of the character's core features, like gender? These decisions involve using language in novel ways, especially around how language choices will be interpreted by an outside audience who may not be intimately familiar with the idiosyncrasies of someone's story.

The advantages of arts practices for language learning are even more pronounced for English learners, specifically around reading comprehension, word retention, and retention of language (Marino, 2018). But there's even better news: Emergent bilinguals—kids who learn two languages simultaneously—participate in the representational trajectory naturally. Bilingual learners are always navigating between the tracks of two expressive media, and live in the space of successive representations in multiple channels that aim at effective communication. They have access to more diverse linguistic resources and have experience moving between languages to meet the needs of different audiences (Spina, 2006). So, bilingual status is a model for the representational trajectories of artmaking, a cultural asset that can be shared through the learning process.

A lovely example of this comes from my colleague Emily Machado, who worked with a 2nd-grade teacher to study how a linguistically diverse group of kids use their language resources to write poetry, what they call "emergent biliteracy" and a "translingual writing" approach (Machado & Hartman, 2019). Kids created poetry using their English writing skills and their oral language skills in their home language, creating poems that show sophisticated attention to audience, purpose, and expression. One poem used English phonological spellings of Urdu words to invoke the importance of culture and religion, while another used Tibetan script transliterated into English words. These poems demonstrate early metarepresentational competence—the capacity to choose the appropriate representational tools for specific concepts. What's incredible to me about this is that the 2nd-graders knew they were leveraging different languages for different communicative purposes and made explicit choices about when to draw on what language. In the arts, language learning is a representational process.

Creativity in Representations. Creativity in education has proven to be an elusive concept that is persistently difficult to define and measure (Kaufman & Sternberg, 2010a). For our purposes, artmaking defines creativity in terms of the translation of ideas into external representations that are then shared with a community. Focusing on representations allows us to track the process and product of creative production and to describe the evolution of ideas as learning.

Kaufman and Sternberg (2010b) describe the three core features of creative ideas: (1) they are *new, different, or innovative*; (2) they are *high quality*; (3) they must be *relevant,* that is, appropriate to the task at hand. The concept of "mini-c" creativity (Beghetto & Kaufman, 2007) is useful here, because it captures what we are after in education, the production and sharing of personally and socially meaningful ideas. Mini-c creativity allows us to take the three key features of creativity—new, high-quality, and relevant—and apply them to personally and locally meaningful contexts:

> We define mini-c creativity as *the novel and personally meaningful interpretation of experiences, actions, and events.* . . . Importantly, the novelty and meaningfulness of these interpretations need not be original or (even meaningful) to others. Indeed, the judgement of novelty and meaningfulness that constitutes mini-c creativity is an intrapersonal judgement. (Beghetto & Kaufman, 2007, p. 73)

According to this definition, something can be new to you and new to your classroom community and qualify as creative. Mini-c also leans into the idea that creativity can be learned and taught; in fact, metarepresentational competence mirrors mini-c creativity, where the goal for participation is to connect ideas to the tools that best allow you to express yourself and to reflect on what you have created.

Arts practices provide a natural opportunity to embed (mini-c) creativity into learning processes. That is because creativity in the arts is making representations grounded in the knowledge and skills of the art form and arts community. Creativity through arts practice in education is learning to use the appropriate tools to express new kinds of understandings. Each representation made by each artist is a creative act because it is a new product that the world has never seen before. For beginning artmakers, learning the tools of a particular artmaking community is the first step toward creative expression. Once learned, artmakers can transcend, or transform, the norms and practices of an art form to expand to representations that develop a new domain of practice. Expressionism, for example, transformed how artists could depict dimensionality in painting, sculpture, and film. Each artmaker is creative in each act of artmaking, and creativity ranges from remixing content and knowledge to producing unique expressions, to the transformation of a whole community and sometimes even the development of entirely new art forms.

In addition to thinking about individuals, groups, and ideas as "creative," it is equally important to understand creativity as a *process* and to understand how the process of creative making is embedded in good teaching and learning (Smith & Smith, 2010). This process is often associated with what learning scientists and engineers call "design thinking," the iterative process involved in planning, creating, testing, and revising ideas and products for a variety of ends, such as coherence, functionality, craft, sustainability for audience, and originality. Design thinking has become an important idea in education, as we push away from learning as content acquisition and toward learning as developing and enacting creative ideas (Razzouk & Shute, 2012). Many artistic disciplines already use design thinking as a mechanism for describing creative processes ranging from architecture to game design to digital storytelling. Both design thinking and artmaking rely on iterative representation as a guide to process: from an initial phase of exploration and ideation—which often involves finding or describing a problem—to the construction of representations (drafts, sketches, or prototypes) that contain potential designs or solutions. From there, we reflect on these through some process, such as critique, and move on to sharing the product either through use, exhibition, sale, gifting, or performance (Halverson & Sheridan, 2014).

Identity

We all agree that identity is an important concept in education (heck, in life), but it has lots of different meanings. We need to look at identity as both a *product*—something that you have—and as a *process*—something that you do. In this way, identity is more about becoming than being. But if we want to reframe education in terms of "doing identity," or "making self," or "becoming a different human," we have to define what we mean by that and how we know it if we see it. Frank captured the importance of identity best when he described how he made his graphic-design piece: "I think it's what artists do. They struggle with what their pieces are about. They struggle with who they are and how they're going to show themselves."

Identity-as-Product: Creating, Doing, and Enacting. Understanding identity as a product of learning allows us to assess the creating, doing, and enacting of identity in the context of artmaking. The art that young people produce represents their identities—it is evidence of how they understand who they are and how they would like to share that understanding with the world. What individuals make represents how they draw on or differentiate themselves from their communities. Art can also represent a collective understanding of identity where development is an expression of community membership. I saw evidence of these forms of creating, doing, and enacting in youth media arts organizations around the country working with young people to create personal, digital art (Halverson et al., 2009).

From an individual perspective, identity looks like a representation of how I see myself, how other people see me, and how I fit into communities (Côté & Levine, 2002). This representation includes socially constructed characteristics, such as class, race, and gender, the kinds of stereotyped images associated with those characteristics, and individuals' more idiosyncratic personal experiences. Arts practices open up the possibility for young people to experiment with their personal and cultural resources in creating representations of identity.

Take the short-form documentary *Rules of Engagement*, which was created through Reel Works Teen Filmmaking in New York City in 2008. The filmmaker describes his movie this way:

> Sometimes, I find it hard to be a good Muslim and an American teenager. My dreams for my future are so different from what my parents want me to do. They think they have better plans for me. Throughout the making of this film, I have learned what being a Muslim is truly about, and I have realized that I am not the only Muslim teen going through this struggle.

Identity is at the intersection of the content of this film and the tools used in filmmaking. In *Rules of Engagement*, the filmmaker inserts his first-person perspective ("here is what I think") into what is otherwise told from a second-person perspective ("here is what you should do"). These perspective shifts are the primary mechanism for depicting the filmmaker's identity because it allows him to directly connect his individualism with the cultural and social ways of being that are part of his Muslim American heritage. As the director of Reel Works told me about the importance of including the filmmaker's perspective in all of the films they produced with young people, "without the 'I' [the films] wouldn't work" (Halverson, 2010a, p. 2371).

The Mizz Perception of Roro! is an autobiographical film about a young African American woman trying to tackle misperceptions about tall women. The film centers on her peers' initial impressions of her, how they've changed over time, and how they connect to her sense of self. Just like *Rules of Engagement*, this filmmaker uses the tools of filmmaking to represent a viable social identity at the intersection of how she sees herself and how others see her. Her use of cinematography as a tool for meaning-making is particularly apparent. She explores the use of extreme angles, first with a bird's eye view shot from Roro's perspective, followed immediately by an upward-tilt shot from the point of view of the person Roro passes on the street. These exaggerated camera angles allow the audience to experience tallness and shortness through film.

The Directors of the Albany Park Theater Project, a youth-arts organization working in a Chicago community, described writing plays as, "opportunities for marginalized or oppressed groups to represent themselves and the world around them as a means of asserting their own identity" (Wiley & Feiner, 2001, p. 122). This can be challenging for young people, as they strive to represent themselves in a way that "accurately" depicts their experiences but does not confirm audiences' stereotypes of historically marginalized communities. Films like *Rules of Engagement* and *The Mizz Perception of Roro!* allow young people who would likely be labeled as "marginalized" or "minoritized" to become agents in shaping the way they create representations of themselves to explore how others interact with their identities.

In the United States, we tend to normalize individualist communities that value autonomy and independence. We therefore tend to see identity as a task of differentiation and transition from our home communities. Films like the ones I just described are great examples of arts-based identity products that value what sets the individual apart from the community. But the arts can also support representations of identity that are about being or becoming a member of a community. Such collectivist communities are interdependent and prioritize shared cultural and social goals (Triandis, 2001). In more collectivist-oriented communities, groups (as opposed to individuals) often help youth determine the topics of youth art and co-compose the products. In collectivist communities, individuals express identity through established roles grounded in the expertise and interest of the group.

A collectivist commitment to identity representation was evident during the time my research team and I spent at Appalshop, an arts and media organization in rural Kentucky that runs programs for local teens. Among the many powerful insights we gleaned was how rural artmaking often focuses on individuals as a part of their communities, highlighting the social, cultural, and historical nature of identity (Pyles, 2016). The short film *Banjo Pickin' Girl*, created in the summer of 2010, is the story of youth participant Stacie Sexton, granddaughter of local banjo legend Lee Sexton.[2] While the 13-minute, 30-second film is "about" Stacie, the story is knitted into her family's narrative and its connections to the history of southeastern Kentucky. Even the title of the film is cultural and historical: The song is a bluegrass classic, originally recorded in 1938 and often performed at music festivals throughout the region. Stacie's story is the story of her family, which is nested in the story of southcentral Kentucky—a collective identity.

Collective identity can be represented in the both the content and the process of artmaking. *In Progress*, a media-arts program in Minnesota, demonstrates how the tools of filmmaking support collectivist identity. The program's director described her understanding of what films represent in the reservation communities in the northern part of the state where she collaborates: A film is both "the story of the individual artist, but also it has this indigenous sense in that it is a collective story of the community and of the people, and of the timelessness of a lot of stories that are within there" (Halverson et al., 2009, p. 32).

Walking Alone on the Road to Depression, a film produced at Leech Lake Reservation in 2001, shows a collective approach to the artmaking process. While the title sounds very individualistic, if you watch the almost 7-minute film, you see how the tools of filmmaking are used as opportunities for representing collective action and identity. The most interesting artistic choice comes about 2:30 in, when we see a first-person point-of-view shot walking into a room. As the camera moves from the doorway to a closeup of the filmmaker under the blankets in her bed, we hear this conversation:

Mom: Get Nikki out of bed . . . Nik, it's almost six o'clock, you gonna get up?
Nikki: (grunts)
Mom: Why not?
Nikki: I don't feel like getting out of bed today.
Mom: Better get up; the day's almost over.
Nikki: (inaudible)
Mom: C'mon the flies are going to get you.

What's interesting about this is that the filmmaker's mom took agency to create footage, and her daughter chose to use the footage in her film. While the topic of the film is about a single person's struggle, the representation of that struggle was created and therefore became an art piece representing a collective experience within the family. While Nikki says she is "walking alone," the film is created together. Artmaking offers mechanisms for valuing both individualist and collectivist identity products.

Identity as Process: Experimenting With and Becoming. Identity is also a process where young people wrestle with difficult ideas, experiment with ways of doing and being, and experiment with new versions of themselves. The psychological concept of "exploring possible selves" is a useful way to understand identity process; possible selves represent peoples' ideas of what they might become, what they would like to become, and what they are afraid of becoming (Markus & Nurius, 1986). Artmaking supports identity exploration by literally allowing artmakers to experiment with new identities. A young actor might play a pregnant teen, a grieving friend, and an abusive parent in the same performance (McLaughlin et al., 1994). Or a person with multiple sclerosis could play an able-bodied person (Wiley & Feiner, 2001). Take, for example, Tino, a young man I worked with at About Face Youth Theater, a program for LGBTQIA+ youth in Chicago creating original ensemble theater (Halverson, 2005). I asked Tino, who identified as a gay man, what it meant for him to play another member of the group, Jane, who identified as transgender. He talked about the transition from feeling incapable of playing someone else to imagining what Jane would feel at a given moment in the scene. This kind of sympathy allowed Tino to open up to the possibility of taking on a different gender identity and to explore this part of himself:

> Then the wig and the dress and the heels, like something happens, like I just come out. And I love it, you know what I mean? It's like putting that on, it's a whole—like I have different pieces of me, of course, but like it's a whole different thing that happens onstage, like it's so liberating.

The concept of exploring possible selves as an identity process in learning captures the playfulness of identity experimentation in both childhood (Goldstein & Lerner, 2018) and adolescence (Halverson, 2005). Teens in particular are always trying on new ways to be, in both individualist and collectivist communities. In my work with first-year college students, I saw how producing radio documentaries served as a site for young artmakers to explore their emerging adulthood, while recognizing the role that their home communities have played in how they see themselves. This was especially complicated for students from minoritized communities at our predominantly white institution. In working with these students to engage in identity process through artmaking, we encouraged them to heed bell hooks's insight: We have choices when we represent ourselves (1999). In an artmaking space, we can choose our audience, which voices to share, which voices to silence, and the language and mode of representation. One of my students, Chris, produced a radio piece that centered on his Jamaican identity and how his parents' journey to America allowed him to become the strong, independent man he is today. Throughout the semester, Chris used the creation of this piece to explore changing identity markers (self-identifying first as Black and then later as Jamaican American), changing positionality (the move from a majority middle-class African American community to a very white university), and his understanding of how blackness is represented at a predominantly white institution (Bass & Halverson, 2013).

One critique of "exploring possible selves" as the model for understanding identity process is that it focuses almost exclusively on the individual. But if we see identity as social and cultural process, and process as participation in arts practice, then we can also see how identity is grounded in the world. Filiberto Barajas-López and Megan Bang (2018) describe how claywork—making with clay—is a deeply historical, cultural, and community-based art form in Indigenous communities. Identity is *in* the arts practice of working clay with your hands, rather than the result of doing the artmaking. Indigenous youth are members of their communities when they make with clay. Artmaking allows for a playful engagement with these resources, as well as the practices and roles of a wider world, to create a flexible space for identity development.

Collaboration

In 2017, I taught a class on becoming a teaching artist for undergraduate and graduate students across the university. Some were enrolled in education programs, while others were from outside our school—sociology, music, dance. All considered themselves practicing artists who were interested in working with nonprofessionals to introduce them to the power of the arts and getting people of all ages excited about making art. I introduced this group of emerging teaching artists to *The Gradual Release of Responsibility* (Fisher & Frey, 2013). The gradual release model suggests that, "the cognitive load should shift slowly and purposefully from teacher-as-model, to joint responsibility, to independent practice and application by the learner" (p. 2). In other words:

> I do it. We do it. You do it.

All Whoopensocker sessions are built on the gradual release model—it is the foundation of our whole-group, small-group, independent approach to self-expression. Fisher and Frey describe this process as recursive and iterative as learners cycle through each set of new tasks. They explain that peer learning ought to be part of the process, so that "you do it" actually includes both "you do it together," and "you do it alone."

> When collaborative learning is done right, our experience suggests that it is during this phase of instruction that students consolidate their thinking and understanding. Negotiating with peers, discussing ideas and information, or engaging in inquiry with others causes students to use what they learned during focused lessons and guided instruction. (2013, p. 7)

This definition seems to indicate that that collaboration is a means to the *real* end, which is for individual kids to display their individual understanding of a particular set of knowledge or skills. In education research, collaboration is often described as a strategy for improving the learning outcomes of individuals. That individualistic perspective bothered my students. When we got into real-life situations where kids were "collaborating," we did not find the end goal beyond the collaborative process to be all that interesting or useful. Instead, we found that the real action of learning happened as the students were collaborating (and learning to collaborate). We began to see collaboration itself as an outcome—a crucially important shift in our thinking about the role of interaction in learning.

In the Fisher and Frey model, "you do it together" precedes "I do it on my own." In our work with kids making art, we often found the reverse to be true. "Collaborative emergence" is a useful way to describe what comes out of groups of people improvising together (Sawyer & DeZutter, 2009). Successful collaborative emergence involves people in making and designing as the goal of learning. In this form of learning, people often take on different roles (or identities, if you will) within the creative process. And, so, individual contributions flow into collaborative-arts practice, and the development of a collaborative identity becomes a desirable outcome. Reframing the process as the outcome helps to build social process into school assessment systems where we almost exclusively measure learning in terms of the individual's standardized achievement. From a collaborative, arts-learning perspective, how boring would it be to ask 30 students to create the same piece of art? And how disingenuous to assume that the function of the collaborative process is for each of these 30 students to work together, then to be evaluated in terms of their separate projects?

Collaboration is both a method and an outcome of the artmaking process. Arts-based learning makes it possible for what we can do together to be legitimate outcomes of learning. There are three ways that we can embrace collaboration as a learning outcome across a range of arts practices: collaboration as productive conflict; as creating new possibilities; and as a pathway to collective ownership.

Collaboration as Productive Conflict. "Productive conflict" is a kind of collaborative emergence that results when groups of kids making art together do not agree. Collaboration is often organized so that the purpose is for kids to negotiate with what they have and know until they come up with a shared answer; remember, "collaborative learning is not the time to introduce new information" (Fisher & Frey, 2013, p. 7). Collaboration as productive conflict, on the other hand, assumes that the art product is richer as a result of the emergence of conflicting views generated during the interaction process, and that this conflict will be embodied in the product itself.

We see this all the time in Whoopensocker, especially as we're working on small-group story writing and performance. Our guiding rule, "every idea is a good idea," means that we are actively encouraging kids to create something that is not a compromise but rather a collective representation. Collective representations can often have discordant features that challenge the audience to make sense of multiple messages carried by the product. And that "good collaboration" doesn't necessarily mean the resolution of conflict but rather a representation of different perspectives. Consider this story, written by 10 4th-graders. This is the one that my friends in the photo from earlier in the chapter performed:

"Infection 2: Dancing Unicorns and the Fortnight Death Scene"

Once upon a time, a unicorn lived in a forest. His name is Sparkletoes. Every day he drinks butterbeer, while watching flying pizzas. One day, a giant unicorn-eating tortoise named Andy walked by—the pet of an evil queen who wanted to kill Sparkletoes. Because of that, she (Sparkle) trotted for her life. Because of that, Sparkletoes runs into Jackson Rudolph, a 15-year-old boy who carries Harry Potter's wand. Jackson protects the unicorn by casting the spell aveda kanara—a killing curse—at the turtle. Ever since that day, unicorns are protected by Jackson or a force field.

In writing together, the kids who signed on as coauthors agreed this narrative collectively represented their ideas. We had eager group members to play Sparkletoes (the infamous Nick) and the evil queen (the almost-as-infamous Gustavo). But there was a kid from the group whose signature was missing. From my journal:

Lamar was hesitant to participate in group writing; he moved from spot to spot in the circle to avoid being called on. But at the end, he insisted "I want to be the good wizard!"—a character that didn't appear in the story. We ended the story [performance] with the appearance of a good wizard, and then he played that character in the performance by himself and with a strong commitment to vocalizing (aha!) and movement (a strong pointing up into the air like he had a sword). He also took his hood off for the performance.

Lamar didn't want to sign his name to the story but did want to participate in the performance, bringing his own character to the mix. The final performance represented a collaborative effort that resulted from the group's conflict, resolved when Lamar received permission (from me and the group) to insert a character into the performance who did not appear in the written story. No one else's contributions were diminished by the addition of the good wizard, and the performance represented a version of the story different from the written one with no ill effects. What we ended up with was collaboration in the form of a written narrative and performance made up of *all* of their knowledge, skills, and creative expression. These art pieces are themselves evidence of productive conflict as learning, and the clashing components of the resulting work give audiences insight into the perspectives of the artist's thinking and collaboration.

Collaboration as Creating New Possibilities. Through their productive conflict, Lamar and his coauthors also generated new possibilities. These new possibilities often result in new knowledge; we see this all the time in maker activities across a range of learning spaces, including libraries, museums, and after-school programs (Halverson et al., 2018; Litts et al., 2020). In one multi-age makerspace in an afterschool program, the instructors challenged participants to build things that illustrated how to "make flow." One young person used a glass jar, cardboard rolls, sugar, tape, and scissors to construct a modified hourglass. Another young maker, seeing what the first person had done, took up the same set of materials and created a charming (but quite fragile!) sugar mill that fit into the city that she was already building. We noticed how similar the use of tools and materials was between these two makers who did not know each other and were not working together.

This similarity in the forms of representation reminded us of a well-known concept from the constructionism world—"collaboration through the air" (Kafai & Harel, 1991). The idea here is that people pick up innovative ideas by being in the same physical space, working with the same tools, materials, and processes, even if they are not working toward the same goal. Collaboration through the air can show how a given design space suggests certain common patterns of ideas and representations. When collected and shown at scale, the surfacing of these patterns can be a powerful tool for creating metarepresentational competence. This idea can be extended to the virtual world: We can't make art together in a pandemic, but we can work synchronously in our own physical spaces. Online sewing circles, real-time chat threads for adapting stories into short movies, and Slack channels that offer opportunities for makers to critique one another's projects are all examples of how collaboration through the air requires synchronous interaction but doesn't require us to be in the same space.

Collaboration as Collective Ownership. Collaboration-as-outcome blurs ownership over the processes and products of artmaking, re-framing learning from what an individual person does to how a collective process actualizes ideas into meaningful representations. I have already talked about how the film *Waking Alone on the Road to Depression* illustrates collectivist conceptions of identity through shared authorship. The film, though it is about "walking alone," is a product of multiple hands, voices, and artists. The maker education world is a great source of examples for collaboration as collective ownership. My colleague Breanne Litts (2015) observed a group of kids who spent the better part of a summer in a public library-based makerspace, cocreating a working foosball table. The adult facilitator described the process this way:

> The foosball table began as one kid's idea supported by his peers and persisted through a collaborative effort in which a couple kids drilled holes, a group of kids painted, still other contributed materials (like action figures), and everyone play tested and refined.

Even though it started as one kid's idea, Breanne describes how it became a collective, community artifact through the design process. Together, they created a scaled-down, cardboard prototype before building a full-scale, usable wood table that they played with and presented at the library's summer maker festival. The kids continued to paint and add action figures while it was on display, signaling that they thought of the work as continuously in progress. The name of the foosball table was "Sunnydale Foosball," though the kid with the original idea felt some ownership over it and woodburned his name into the table. When Breanne asked him why he did this, he replied: "They'll be like, 'this is awesome! Who made this?' And then I'll be like, 'me!'" In this way, individual learning and collaborative outcomes coexist, reminding us that individuals can identify an artifact as evidence of their own learning, even as the artifact itself represents a collaborative outcome.

This is revolutionary for the classroom. Shifting from a means to an end changes collaboration into something we want young people to learn to do as a learning process—not just a vehicle to learn content. Learning to collaborate means generating productive conflict, creating new possibilities, and seeing these new possibilities as collaborative. The processes and products themselves serve as evidence for collaboration, and arts practices show the way for how we can bring learning outcomes in all of our classrooms.

REPRESENTATIONS + IDENTITY + COLLABORATION = LEARNING!

The learning outcomes that result from artmaking are all linked to one another through representation, identity, and collaboration. Nick's participation in Whoopensocker was marked by a series of collaborative, representational acts, which are themselves outcomes of his participation. His argument about whether dreams are important is coauthored; Nick and his aide not only worked together but offered contrasting opinions to create an authentic argument. The unicorn horns used in the classroom performance of "Dancing Unicorns and the Fortnight Death Scene" were Nick's invention, but then everyone decided to make and use them. These collaborative outcomes are also identity claims. The text of his dreams argument, "Nick believes this," a collective story with multiple signatures, and Lamar's surprise wizard appearance are all identity claims. Further, these identity claims are all clearly representations that use a range of tools to communicate ideas. Language development is loudly and proudly on display. Nick and Gustavo's progress from "not saying anything" to active writers and performers is a big developmental step in 6 weeks. Imagine what they could do if they were engaged in these practices all the time!

My goal is for us to take what we learn in and from arts practices and re-center these outcomes as the essential features of good learning in and out of schools. The arts allow us to reclaim concepts like failure, cheating, and plagiarism as important and necessary components of any learning process. If our learning outcomes are focused on individual demonstration of knowledge and skills in a particular discipline, then failure represents a "lack of learning" and is a very real possibility for many kids. But if we refocus our efforts on the construction and refinement of representations, engagement with identity process and product, and collaborative work, it is hard to see how failure is even an option. Same with plagiarism. If we expect that outcomes are connected to what people bring—representational, linguistic, identity resources—and that the art they make re-mixes the collective of resources, we no longer need to worry about "copying" or "cheating." Instead, copying and cheating become valued learning strategies—strategies like collaboration through the air, experimenting with possible selves, and developing a critical team. For the past 20 years, I have studied closely how learning happens in arts practices. I am now proposing a new frame for learning grounded in the three most important processes of human learning: representation, identity, and collaboration.

CHAPTER 4

Improvisation as the Model for Good Teaching

My all-time favorite musical track on any album is the live recording of Stevie Wonder's "Ribbon in the Sky" from 1995's *Natural Wonder*. With a minute to go on the more than 8-minute track, he wraps up a long jam session by singing a short, joyous "Ribbon in the Sky!" He is about to continue with the next line, "for our love," when a group of audience members responds with, "ribbon in the sky!" Stevie gets as far as "for," and then stops short to take in their response. "Oh, okay," he says, and sings a different variation of the "Ribbon in the Sky" lyric for the audience to repeat. His call-and-response evolves, as he sings different lyrics to the same tune: "yeah, yeah, yeah, yeah, yeah" and "hey, hey, hey, hey, hey." After five exchanges with the audience, he finishes the song solo.

The reason I continually return to this performance—and this moment—as a touchstone is that in the split second it takes Stevie to *hear* what his audience is giving him, to acknowledge it, to incorporate it, and to make it a part of the performance, he has created a large-scale learning moment. This is constructivism at its most public and most literal; the ability to read what another person (or thousands of people) are giving you, to understand where they are in the meaning-making process, and to actively bring that meaning-making into the cocreation of something new is the ultimate teachable moment. The improvisation that happens over the span of this 26 seconds inspires my work.

In this moment, Stevie is teaching. This form of teaching is based on the features of artistic improvisation, and it points to a method for teachers to make learning possible for all kids. Since we are committed to learning as creating and sharing collaborative representations that are focused on identity, we need an equivalent theory of teaching that makes these learning outcomes possible. Enter improv, stage left.

WHAT IS IMPROV?

For many people "improv" is a four-letter word. I know, I know, improv is a five-letter word. Literalists. People are scared of improv, because it either makes them think of comedy ("I can't just stand there, and make up jokes!"), or because they think that there are no rules ("Doesn't improv mean do whatever you want?"). These are both myths. Improvisation (improv) is a particular form of artmaking that stretches across performance media, including theater, music, and dance (Sawyer, 2011). In this way, improv is both its own art form and a genre of artmaking that stretches across forms. Improv in theater can refer to a process for making art, a set of tools used by actors to work on characters and scenes for performance. It's also a performance medium that relies on a range of forms that actors use to produce scenes, songs, and monologues on the spot. Within the performance genre, improv can be characterized as sketch-based, short-form, or long-form (Leep, 2008). And, yes, sometimes those scenes are funny; the most famous improvisers are comedians, so I understand where that misconception comes from. But most comedy—stand-up, sketch—is *highly* scripted. Most of your favorite comedians don't just make that stuff up on the spot.

Before we go further, let's look at some definitions from other scholarship on the role of improv in education. Keith Sawyer, a scholar of learning theory and creativity, has done some great research on teaching as an improvisational activity. In his 2011 book, *Structure and Improvisation in Creative Teaching*, he frames improvisation this way:

> Improvisation is generally defined as a performance (music, theater, or dance), in which performers are not following a script or score, but are spontaneously creating their material as it is performed. Improvisation can be as basic as a performer's elaboration or variation of an existing framework—a song, melody, or plot outline. At the other extreme, in some forms of improvisation, the performers start without any advance framework and create the entire work on stage. (pp. 11–12)

Among education folks, early childhood scholars are the most open to embracing improv as a model for understanding play as good teaching (Graue et al., 2015; Jurow & McFadden, 2005; Lobman, 2006). That we see these ideas taken up primarily in early childhood education should come as no surprise. Sadly, the idea that learning should involve play is only acceptable with our youngest learners. Once we hit elementary school, play becomes an alternative to learning. It's something we do when we need a break from the real, serious work of getting an education. This is clearly not something I espouse, but definitely part of the broader discourse on what counts as "good" education. Even worse, play is disappearing from early childhood education at an alarming rate. Now, every year of schooling is constructed as preparation for the years that follow. But if we reimagine teaching through the lens of improv, we can "age up" play, and bring joy back to all learning environments.

In short, improv is:

Collaborative: By definition, improv requires people to work together. While individuals can create spontaneously on their own, improv requires more than one person to create something new. This is true of all human interaction, but we often forget that when we think about the act of teaching. If we see learning as collaboration, it makes sense that teaching must also be collaborative.

Emergent: What gets made in improv is never set in advance. The performance, whether for an audience or for the performers themselves, is a result of interactions that are not decided ahead of time. This is also something we forget when we think about teaching.

Connected to identity: Our identities are, in part, a result of internal psychological mechanisms as well as the ways in which we act when we are with other people. In a "you are what you eat" sort of way, we become the things we do and say. Since improv involves creating new ideas through interaction, identities get made in the process.

IMPROV IS GOOD TEACHING

In my pre-education days, I trained as an actor and an improviser. I came up in Chicago in the 1990s, in the shadow of Second City, where resident geniuses Tina Fey, Amy Poehler, Rachel Dratch, and others cut their teeth on short-form and long-form comedy improvisation. Even before these hilarious women became famous, my friends and I wanted to be them. Tina Fey is especially brilliant in how she talks about what improv is and what it does. There is a great two-page callout in her 2011 memoir, *Bossypants*, aptly titled, "Rules of Improvisation That Will Change Your Life and Reduce Belly Fat." In it, she describes improv, "not only as a way of creating comedy but as a worldview." This is the foundation for how I describe the features of improv, woven together with ideas of other folks who have thought about the role of improv in education. All of it helped me to redefine good teaching.

Rule 1: "The First Rule of Improvisation Is Agree"

As you know from the Whoopensocker agreements, every idea is a good idea. This agreement is about saying yes to yourself, to your classmates, to your teaching artists, and to your classroom teachers. While I didn't hear that from Tina first, her rules of improv, which begin with "say yes," are a useful place to start. "The Rule of Agreement reminds you to 'respect what your partner has created' and to at least start from an open-minded place. Start with a YES and see where that takes you" (Fey, 2011, p. 84). Early childhood educator Carrie Lobman calls that the "giving and receiving of offers" (2006). What that means in an improv scene is that you never deny what your partner has created. It does *not* mean that you can never use the word "no," or disagree. Rather, it means that you don't negate what your partner has created by pretending it's not there.

A Whoopensocker favorite for teaching kids to say, "yes" is the four-line improv scene. First, we brainstorm characters and settings as a whole group. Then two teaching artists take suggestions from the character list and improvise two exchanges of dialogue and movement. A third person writes this down, so that students can be invited up to re-enact this mini-play. Eventually, kids volunteer to be assigned characters to create their own improvised four-line dialogues. We (hopefully) see this in traditional classroom activities all the time. Take debate in a social studies classroom; the goal of debate is not for everyone to agree on everything. But a goal for debaters is to acknowledge an argument, and then directly affirm or refute that argument. Debaters can disagree as a way to respect what their partner—in this case a fellow debater—has created.

Saying "yes" is about a constructivist approach to teaching and learning. Since new knowledge is always built on already existing knowledge, experiences, and practices, people can't learn something new unless they see how it is connected to something they already know. We have all had (or maybe even been) that teacher who says in response to a student's answer to our question, "No, that's not exactly what I meant." Or, "Who else has an idea to contribute?" Both of these acknowledgments are negations. By saying "no" to an offer, we effectively sever that link for students, and tell them that they need totally new information or ways of thinking to be able to answer our question correctly. Of course, the answer can be wrong, especially if the question is informational or asked for the purpose of summarizing. Saying "yes" reminds us that our job as teachers is not to elicit the right answer but, rather, to build connections for learners between what they bring to the learning environment and what you want them to get out of it. It reminds us that our basic interactions with students ought to be around understanding how they're contributing and why they're choosing to contribute that way. There are lots of methods for getting at student perspectives that can both result in "wrong" answers, and help students build connections between their understanding and documented factual information. Requiring multiple sources of evidence, for example. If you're going to ask a student when an event took place, they can use their peers and the Internet at the same time to arrive at a shared answer.

Rule 2: Say, "Yes, And . . . "

While saying "yes" means affirming that students have contributed ideas to your learning space, it does not mean you have to always agree with what they say. Answers can be straight up incorrect. As the teacher, you do not have to let their incorrect answer go unchecked, because you are afraid it will sound too much like a no. This is where "yes, and" comes in. "The second rule of improvisation is not only to say yes, but YES, AND. You are supposed to agree, and then *add something* of your own. . . . YES, AND means don't be afraid to contribute" (Fey, 2011, p. 84). In an improv scene, adding something of your own moves the scene along. The purpose of a scene is to get from point A to point B, even though you don't know in advance what those two points are. But movement is not possible if no one contributes new information, and it is much more difficult if only one person is doing so. The most skilled improvisers make it look as if they are not doing anything, while their choices continue to move the scene along. "Yes, and" signals to the people you are improvising with that you are listening. Teacher-educators Lisa Barker and Hilda Borko call this "presence," and they map how that concept is a way to describe good improv and good teaching through three features: connection to themselves, attunement to others, and knowledge of subject matter (2011). The key to "yes, and" is the insight that arts-based learning is always a dialogue. Each artistic product or performance is built to participate in a larger discourse, in which the artist receives feedback from the audience, and the audience learns from the work of the artist. Adding the ". . . and" into Rule 2 builds discourse into the foundation of improv by requiring participants to continue the connection chain with each other's representations.

While I think the idea of telling students to say "yes, and . . ." is fairly well accepted (we are *always* telling students to collaborate and the often-dreaded group project is grounded in this insight), teachers should make it a regular part of their practice too. When teachers model the "yes, and . . ." method, then students can learn how collaboration can lead to real constructivist learning with each other. That is the logic behind the Whoopensocker model. Taking what kid authors have created and bringing professional actors, comedians, and musicians to the table is not cheating. It's part of the process. Group story writing is an excellent format for encouraging "yes, and" among artists. Without it, the world would not have the gift of, "The man who passed out who did not go to jail, *or* the concert that ended 15 minutes early." Here's a pro tip: If you truly value the contributions students are making, then they will be interested and willing to hear your contributions as well. This kind of "yes, and . . ." allows everyone in the room, including the teacher, to contribute and to value individual expertise on the path to collective output.

Rule 3: Make Statements

A common misinterpretation of a constructivist perspective on learning is that teachers can never tell students anything, ever. All information must be discovered, or it can't be constructed. Since learning is discovery, pedagogy must also be discovery. Cognitive psychologist Rich Mayer (2004) calls this the "constructivist teaching fallacy," and provides lots of empirical evidence that having students discover everything for themselves is not very effective. There is a robust debate (as aggressive as you'll get with learning theorists) about whether the problem is constructivism as a theory or how constructivism has been interpreted as a way of doing teaching (see Kirschner, 2006 & Hmelo-Silver et al., 2007, for an exciting exchange!).

What does improv have to do with the discovering vs. telling pedagogy debate? According to Tina Fey, "The next rule is MAKE STATEMENTS . . . Whatever the problem, be part of the solution. Don't just sit around raising questions and pointing out obstacles" (p. 84). As teachers, a big part of our role is knowing where and when to place the cognitive load (as in, who is doing the heavy lifting, thinking-wise). Figuring out who should take the cognitive load is constantly happening in an improvised scene; this is as much a marker of an effective teacher as it is of an effective improviser. Tina reminds us that always asking questions as a method of refusing the cognitive load can be frustrating and can stop forward progress in a scene. As a teacher, you would be disingenuous to pretend you don't know the answer to a question. And, yet, it's a go-to in the classroom; rather than "giving" students information, we often suggest it in the form of questions. Instead of using questions as a pedagogical tool, I find that offering what I know is an invitation to move our collective work forward. In addition, it takes the pressure off of students to "know the right answers" and instead distributes the cognitive load evenly across learners and educators.

Rule 4: "There Are No Mistakes, Only Opportunities"

I want to start with Tina's example, as it is especially evocative here:

> If I start a scene as what I think is very clearly a cop riding a bicycle, but you think I am a hamster in a hamster wheel, guess what? Now, I'm a hamster in a hamster wheel. I'm not going to stop everything to explain that it was really supposed to be a bike. Who knows? Maybe I'll end up being a police hamster who's been put on "hamster wheel" duty, because I'm "too much of a loose cannon" in the field. (p. 85)

Making the most of what your partner says means reframing key parts of their statements in order to keep the conversation rolling. This refers us back to our old friend constructivism: since learners always use prior knowledge to make sense of new ideas, when their conceptual understanding does not match ours, telling them "no," and giving them the right answer just gives a new piece of information—it does not address their prior understanding. Teachers can use this rule to fit new information to already existing information so that learners can understand the new connections and rebuild their prior concepts. Any good conceptual change theorist will tell you that. Also, learners don't just make up random answers to questions. When you ask a learner a question, that person gives you an answer that they think makes sense even if their sensemaking is an act of resistance. So, cognitively, a mistake (or an act of resistance) needs to be seen as an opportunity.

A few years ago, during a Whoopensocker residency, I was working with Dimonte, a 3rd-grader who was an enthusiastic participant in group story writing and performance activities but turned sullen as soon as everyone got the chance to do independent writing in their journals. "Sullen" presents in a lot of ways. Sometimes, a kid will sit at their desk with their notebook closed and their head down. Passive resistance. This usually means that they are nervous about the act of writing, that the motor coordination required either slows them down or stops them completely. In these cases, offering to write while a kid talks through their story, or starting the physical writing process for them can be enough to give permission to express ideas.

Dimonte, however, was engaged in active resistance. Sitting on the floor, knees up, hunched over with pencil in hand, he was meticulously making a giant "X" on every page of his notebook, one page at a time. (In improv speak, we might call this "a mistake" since he was definitely not doing the task that was assigned.) I knelt down and watched him for a minute. He looked up at me, not pausing in his X-making, daring me to scold him for not doing what he was told, or to tell him that he was "ruining his notebook." Devilishly clever, since he was technically writing, so if I tried to scold him, he could tell me he *was* doing what he was told. Instead, I said, "Hey, that's cool. Can I see it for a second?" While I wasn't sure what I wanted to write, I knew that I wanted to use his active resistance somehow, to validate the work he was doing as connected to the work that I was hoping he would do. I took one of the pages and used the space in each of the four Vs made by the shape of the letter X to write in the widest part:

Something I am good at . . .
Something that is fun . . .
Something that is boring . . .
Something I am scared of . . .

I handed the journal back to him and said, "I bet you can't fill in this X with words."

"Pfffft, yes I can," he said, turning the paper around, so he could read each of the prompts. Under each, he wrote:

Nothing
Nothing
Nothing
Nothing

"You're not scared of anything?!" I asked him incredulously.

"Nope."

"I am scared of a ton of stuff," I said, honestly.

"Not me," Dimonte told me.

"Well, what are all the things that you are not scared of?" I asked him. "Can you write them down? I want you to share with everyone all the stuff you're not scared of, and I don't think you'll remember it if you don't write it down."

Dimonte flipped to one of the pages in his journal that didn't have a giant X scrawled across it and wrote this:

I'm not scared of anything.
I am not scared of clowns.
I am not scared of spiders.
I am not scared of Colin.[1]
I am not scared of anybody. I am not scared of a jackhammer.
I am not scared of a gun.

Dimonte and I used his "mistake" as an opportunity to create something, working together by building on each other's ideas. A coda to this story: We chose to perform "I'm Not Scared" in the show at Dimonte's school and, again, for our end-of-the-year extravaganza for the public. Putting Dimonte's piece into our professional performance is another form of turning an act of resistance into an opportunity for production and performance.

Seeing mistakes as opportunities is a teaching strategy that values failure as an integral, necessary part of learning. I have already talked about how the arts allow us to reclaim failure as a component of the learning process; seeing mistakes as opportunities is the method for working with learners to do so. Unfortunately, in modern schooling discourse, we use "failure" to describe the state of not doing something right, of not learning. We apply the word to schools, to teachers, and, of course, to students. The phrase "failing schools" is a pretty popular form of alarmist-speak, used as clickbait to get folks riled up about the poor state of American teaching and learning. This discourse is especially destructive in the classroom environment, because it constructs learning as binary (you are a good student, or you aren't; you did well on the test, or you didn't), rather than as a process of doing and becoming. By seeing mistakes as opportunities, teachers and students can ask of a learning process, "What happened here?" "What did I mean to have happen?" "How do these two things line up and how don't they?"

Why I Love Rules

The best thing about these four rules is that they are, in fact, rules, dispelling the myth that anything goes in improv. Anything does not go (sorry, Cole Porter!)—educators must always say, (1) "yes,"; (2) say "yes and . . ."; (3) make statements, and (4) see mistakes as opportunities. The most basic comedy improv game, freeze tag, involves two people make up a scene together until a third person yells "freeze" and takes the place of one of the original two. A new scene starts from the position they just took over. It sounds super intimidating and seems as if you could say literally anything. And I suppose you could. But people don't; they say one of a relatively few set of things. And the position they freeze in further constrains what they say and do. Do you know how many times I saw a person take over the position of a person sitting down with their hands on their knees who started the new scene with, "The baby's coming!" At least 100. And I'm not even close to a professional improviser. Those folks have probably seen the birthing scene 10,000 times.

The same is true in teaching. While it is true that a child can say or do literally anything in response to a question you pose, a provocation you make, or a set of materials you offer up—they won't. They will say one of about six things and the longer you teach, the more likely you will be to recognize in advance what those six things might be so you can be prepared. Beth Graue, an early childhood warrior who continues to hold the line for play as the way we ought to think about our interactions with young kids, studies how teachers of 4-year-old kindergarteners use improv in their classrooms. She refers to this constrained set of responses as "scripts" that are a "joint endeavor" between teachers and learners (Graue et al., 2015). Unlike the "scripted curriculum," where teachers and students are given words to say by a curriculum developer that they may not deviate from (*shiver*—this is not what I'm talking about), these scripts are cocreated in the moment *but* familiar and predictable, based on the context, the content, and the people.

Research on teaching in different subject areas has done a great job of helping us understand what a constrained set of learner moves might look like. A well-known example of this comes from cognitive psychologists Stella Vosniadou and William Brewer, who conducted a series of studies on what young children understand about the shape of the Earth (1992). Their team interviewed hundreds of kids and found that all of the kids gave one of six different explanations for why we experience the Earth as flat while we know that it is round. Some give the scientific explanation, talking about gravity, heliocentrism, size, or atmosphere. Some straight-up just say that the Earth is flat. In between, kids say that the Earth is round but flat like a pancake, or that it's round but flat on the four surfaces we live on, or that it's round, but that there is a hole in the top, and inside is a flat disc that we live on, or that there are two Earths: the one we live on and the one in the sky. That's it. Six things. Six scripts that contain the total possible theories that children offer when they make sense of this pretty complicated scientific idea. So, every time we teach a group of people something, we get a little closer to knowing that when you play freeze tag, someone is probably going to try to give birth, and when you teach earth science, someone is probably going to hear you say, "the Earth is round," and think, "Hmmm. Now, that's an Earth I've never been on before."

Improv is a way to access and work with the range of understandings that learners bring to each situation. In their study of two kindergarten/1st-grade teachers, Jurow and Creighton McFadden (2005) show how students can come to understand science phenomena through disciplined improvisation. Disciplined, because in their words, "teachers build on students' ideas in order to connect them to disciplinary concerns, concepts, and discursive practices" (p. 237). Improvisation is the structure that connects students' knowledge to science ideas and practices. Mathematically speaking, student ideas + improvisation = science learning!

WHAT DOES TEACHING-AS-IMPROV LOOK LIKE?

Now, applying these rules to a teaching setting is nontrivial. It's not as if we can say, "Well, that's done! We've fixed teaching by understanding the four simple rules of improvisation that will change your life. I want to shift from defining the rules to describing how these rules get applied in practice and what it looks like when we do.

Scaffold the Risk, Y'all

The key to all good teaching, which I have learned from years of making art with people of all ages, is to scaffold risk-taking for everyone involved. If you have ever worked with me, you've heard me say, "Scaffold the risk!" I've even heard former students, friends, and colleagues use this phrase in their own instruction. So, this is my chance to put the Halverson stamp on it. You heard it here: The key to good teaching is scaffolding risk-taking. Let's spend a little time on each of these two words, as they're both important.

First, *scaffolding.* Scaffolding is an education idea that uses the metaphor of a temporary structure used in construction to give builders a place to work and to make sure a new building doesn't collapse before it is ready to stand on its own. Roy Pea's excellent essay (2004) reviews the history of scaffolding in education research and gives us some key features to attend to:

- Scaffolding is both a *social process* and a *set of tools.* Sometimes, it's hard to tell the difference between the two, but it's important to recognize that we can find scaffolding in both designed artifacts (like a computer program) or interactions (like a conversation with a teacher).
- Scaffolding must *fade.* Just like the temporary structures on a construction site, the point of the scaffolding is to take it away when you don't need it anymore. If it's permanent, it's not scaffolding, it's part of the building.
- *Channeling, focusing,* and *modeling* are the three mechanisms for scaffolding learners' experiences. We set up rules to focus the work, point out relevant features, then demonstrate how we do this work as more experienced collaborators.

I am not the first person to talk about the importance of scaffolding as a critical part of teaching. What is different here is that I use the concept of scaffolding not for learning specific content but as a necessary part of any successful learning environment.

Without scaffolding, *risk-taking* becomes very expensive. I have dedicated this chapter to arguing that what we do when we teach is improvise. And I acknowledged that many, many people get afraid when they hear the word *improv.* Why? Because it is a huge risk to "put yourself out there" in a scene, and make stuff up as you go along, hoping it makes sense and that people like it. The exact same thing is true of teaching and learning. One of the main reasons that people don't volunteer ideas in a group setting is that they are afraid of being wrong. Many classrooms are dominated by a small group of voices who take all the risks and are always heard. This kind of classroom can evolve into fixed camps of participants where the cognitive load is not shared evenly across learners, This is especially true for students who are trained to think that the purpose of questions and activities in school is to figure out the right answer. (Given that, it makes sense why improv is employed most frequently in early childhood classrooms where kids have not yet figured out that the purpose of their contributions in class is to be judged for their correctness.)

But it's not just students who have to learn to take risks in the classroom. Teachers also have to learn to take risks. It is terrifying to stand up in front of a group of people who expect you to be the expert on something they probably do not want to learn anyway, and to find yourself saying, "I don't know; let's see if we can figure that out together." But students need to learn how to take the risk of trying out new ideas, and saying, "I don't know," so teachers need to lead the way. Risk-taking thrives on trusting relationships. Even though I love to make new ideas with people, I am less willing to do that in a room where (1) I don't know anyone, and (2) we are not organized to work comfortably together. Whenever I work with teachers-in-training, I always start with improv games, specifically the kinds of games that scaffold risk so that participants don't have to make public, independent choices right away. Call-and-response games, where I do something silly, and then everyone else does the same silly thing back, are the perfect way to start the risk-taking process.

In the beginning, the teacher has to take on the risk of carrying the cognitive load so that it can be continued through the rest of the learning process. My favorite improv stretch involves reaching up as high as you can, and then relaxing, one body part at a time. When I get to the part where our arms are relaxed but shoulders still tensed, I say, "Okay, now, walk like Frankenstein," and start walking like the famous monster, while making a moaning sound. At first, students are surprised. They laugh. Sometimes genuinely, and sometimes uncomfortably. It's a laugh, so I don't care. But as we repeat the stretching sequence, more and more people jump into the "walk like Frankenstein" moment. After five rounds, almost everyone is doing it. And those who aren't know that I set the tone of silliness and unpredictability as a way to scaffold risk in the rest of our interactions.

About teaching improv as an art form, Jeanne Leep says: "When your students . . . understand that you are experimenting, that you are willing to take risks yourself, then the expectation of 'expert' is removed from the work, and the group will take more ownership of the process" (2008, p. 134). It can be upsetting for teachers to let go of being an "expert"; the rules of improv can scaffold that change in the power dynamic. Adults are paid to be in charge, and many newer teachers use that role status to bolster what they think they are supposed to be doing in the classroom. But it's not just teachers who are uncomfortable losing the expert moniker. Because students have also participated for a long time in places where the expert-novice scaffold was used, they can also find it upsetting when they think the teacher is not in charge or doesn't know everything. When students are socialized to believe that their teachers have all the answers they can find transgressive behavior more attractive than real questions. We need risk-taking to debunk the myth of the teacher as all-knowing expert. And what better way to do that than playing improv games that move groups from responding to leader-initiated silliness to creating their own scenes where the outcome is unpredictable?

Scaffolding risk is the single most important teacher move in the arsenal of creating a productive learning environment, whether it's an arts-based environment or a traditional classroom. Let me say it louder for those of you in the back: NO ONE CAN LEARN IF THEY ARE NOT WILLING TO BE WRONG, AND YOU WON'T BE WILLING TO BE WRONG IF YOU DON'T TAKE A RISK.[2] And when we think about risk-taking in terms of improv, as Beth Graue and colleagues remind us, "Using the lens of improv to study teacher–child interactions shifts the focus away from what the teacher is doing and towards what the teacher and children are doing together" (p. 456). When we think about teaching and learning as improv, producing knowledge becomes a joint task rather than a scary, individual, isolated act. In theater, we call it being a member of an ensemble. In education, we call it "joint-knowledge construction."

Instruction Is Distributed

Scaffolding risk requires us to abandon the traditional power dynamic of the single, adult expert as the primary source of knowledge in the classroom. In the 1990s, as we embraced a more student-centered model of learning, there was a popular rhetorical shift around the teacher—from "sage on the stage" to "guide on the side" (King, 1993). While this was a good start, a guide on the side still maintains the teacher as the sole adult expert in the space. And Keith Sawyer (2011) points out that when we use performance as a metaphor for good teaching, we often end up reinforcing the solo-expert idea (when we say expert performance, who doesn't think of a Hamlet soliloquy?).

There are surprisingly few academic studies that identify alternative instructional models that decenter the single-expert teacher. In fact, the most popular theories of teacher expertise—most notably *pedagogical content knowledge*—emphasize how the teacher should have all of the knowledge and skills for effective teaching. Since I entered this game as a teaching artist, I have always worked with others who provide expertise that I can't; the focus on the single, adult expert surprised me. Conducting research allowed me to study how teaching happens in arts-based spaces and to figure out a way to talk about a new model for teaching. And, thus, was born "a theory of distributed instruction" (Halverson et al., 2015). Sounds familiar, right? If we buy that cognition is distributed, it comes with a side order of instruction.

We developed the theory of distributed instruction while working with youth media-arts organizations around the United States—in New York, Chicago, Whitesburg, Kentucky, and an Ojibwe reservation in northern Minnesota. You have already heard a little about the art that was produced during the time we spent in these organizations: Frank's graphic-design representation of himself as border crosser, along with the films *Walking Alone on the Road to Depression*, *Banjo Pickin' Girl*, *Rules of Engagement*, and *The Mizz Perception of Roro!* were all made in these organizations. We studied each organization through one production cycle, from the first day young people walked into the space until the day they shared the digital art they had made. They produced work that included documentary and narrative films, photography, graphic art, and audio art. Across all of them, we found that arts-based learning environments function as distributed instructional systems, where teaching is stretched across people, tools, activities, and time. Here is an example of distributed instruction in action, taken directly from our observation notes, during our time at the Street Level Youth Media program in Chicago. We refer to the teachers as "mentors" here, because that is what they were called in this program:

> Breana edits raw media footage for her documentary, with the help of three different instructors across an hour-long editing session. She downloads some found footage and is about ready to start editing. The first mentor offers Breana the technical expertise necessary to complete the initial task of transferring footage into Final Cut Pro, helping her with the capture. When she figures out the technical element, he extracts himself saying, "So, I'll let you just start, and you let me know if you need anything." She calls him back over immediately and asks about a red line that appeared above her editing in Final Cut Pro. He explains that this is about rendering. He walks away, again, and she continues editing. About 10 minutes later, a second mentor comes over and listens to some of the interview Breana has recorded. She asks Breana if she has an idea of where she is going with it and if this is going to be part of the final project. Breana says, "Yes," and the mentor says she's glad to hear that and praises the interview. She reminds Breana to consider the audience for the piece, as she begins the editing process. In this context, Breana makes an editing choice, choosing the transition from her grandfather to her grandmother as her grandmother's comment, "I married an older man" plays on the screen. Breana is happy with this transition and continues clipping audio. A few minutes pass with Breana editing, then a third mentor interrupts, "Can I just show you this?" and she shows Breana how to zoom in using Final Cut. She sits down with Breana who asks, "Can I crop it here?" and she shows Breana how to do it. Then she asks what Breana is planning to do with the footage. Breana repeats her plans to use it as a final project, and the mentor asks if she can hear what Breana has so far. She listens to the editing. After she listens, she says, "Great, you've got to leave, 'I married an older man,' that is such a good transition." Breana thanks her, and the third mentor shows her how to use the audio-balancing tool to even out the audio. She demonstrates it, then she says, "I'll take it out and let you decide." Breana thanks her, again, and says, "Yeah, I think I'll do that later." (July, 2008)

What should you notice about Breana's editing process and how it proceeded in these moments? First, each of the three mentors provided different kinds of instruction: Mentors One and Three contribute to Breana's technical skills but in different ways. Mentor Two plays a framing role, helping Breana to consider the purpose of her work but does not provide any technical support. Second, Breana was using several technological tools as instructors. She was working with Final Cut Pro video-editing software, learning different features by trying them out. She was also using the Internet to both find footage and to get information for how to import this footage into her piece. The sum of these interactions provided the support necessary for Breana to engage meaningfully in the editing process. In this example, instruction was distributed across three mentors and two technological tools.

Distributed cognition is pretty well accepted among learning theorists who study everything from schools to workplaces. So, it has always felt strange to me that it has not made its way into instruction. To be fair, most traditional schools are organized around a model where instruction is distributed to different subject-matter experts within and across grades. However, these models often lack the sense of learner-focused, collaborative work toward a shared project that marks arts-based learning spaces. In other words, we are cool with the idea that knowing is stretched across people and tools and time, but *what we need to know* is still thought of as the property of adult, all-knowing experts who are responsible for the content, pedagogy, and design of their students' experiences. We need to extend the distributed metaphor to classrooms; that model is already at work in the systems of arts-based teaching and learning.

The description of Breana editing her video is one of literally thousands of examples of how young people learn to make art through distributed instruction. It makes sense, right? We already know that artmaking is itself a distributed cognitive endeavor. Keith Sawyer calls it *collaborative emergence*, meaning that collaboration itself is the outcome and what this outcome looks like is not fixed before the group comes together to make something (Sawyer & deZutter, 2009). Collaborative emergence results from a distributed cognitive process where people use the tools of their artistic medium (e.g., dance steps, musical phrases) to create a shared whole (e.g., a choreographed piece). Arts processes are, by definition, distributed, and we can learn a lot about how to structure instruction in a distributed way by looking at how arts practices do this.

A common refrain I hear is—"Oh, that all sounds great, but that could *never* happen in my school!" "Well, consider," I reply, "the many examples of classroom teacher/teaching artist partnerships that happen every day." We can see this in action at the Digital Youth Network (DYN), a collection of in-school and out-of-school programs coupled with a virtual-learning platform designed to allow predominantly African American kids from the South Side of Chicago access to the broadest possible range of spaces, tools, and people (Barron et al., 2014). Teaching artists serve as both the primary mentors to young people in the out-of-school space and collaborators with classroom teachers who are interested in bringing arts practices into the classroom. Their work provides a roadmap for how educators can design for distributed instruction (Richards et al., 2014).

WHAT DO WE DO NOW?

The title of this chapter is a big claim: that the arts are the answer to how we ought to think about good teaching. Well, here it is. In looking at teaching through an arts lens, we can see that teaching is improvisation, and improvisation is both collective and risky. Improvisatory teaching *does not* mean anything goes. Tina's rules give us a clear framework for what it means to do good teaching—say, "Yes," say "Yes . . . and," "Make statements," and "No mistakes, only opportunities"—are clear foundations for how to structure interactions with students. And here's the good news: We are not alone. If we earnestly take up these rules, it means that teaching becomes a collective act that is distributed across people and tools and time. We can abandon the (often isolating and scary) idea that a teacher must be an all-knowing, all-doing person in order to be successful. Use the other adults around you. Use students' ideas and expertise. Use the tools in the environment. All of it is fair game, and together we can build new knowledge.

However! (it's a big "however," that's why it gets an exclamation point)—to be successful, everyone in the learning environment must be willing to take risks. Everyone. Never ask your students to do something that you would never do yourself. If you want silly, you have to be willing to act silly. If you want students to give something of themselves, you have to be willing to give something of yourself. If you want authentic products, you have to be a creator, too. And, if you don't know how to choreograph a dance? Learn how alongside your students. Do the work. It will mean you take the risk. And! (Here's the "Yes, and" part.) Improvisation in the arts provides scaffolding for risk-taking. No one has to dive right into the deep end. We are building a zero-entry swimming pool here.

Most importantly, we can use these ideas to engage students who are currently disconnected from formal education and transform our schools to better meet the needs of all of our learners. These ideas should resonate with current teaching practice and prompt us to change so we try out more emergent, risk-taking learning environments. From my perspective, that's the ballgame.

CHAPTER 5

Reimagining Curriculum Through the Lens of Design

Whoopensocker teaching artists begin the playwriting day of our residency by improvising a short play based on characters, a setting, and a problem that kids suggest. This is the "I do" portion of the gradual release model. Then comes the "we do" portion, where kids act out our improvised words. Finally, the "you do together"—pairs and trios of kids come up with their own short plays and perform them for the class. We have been using this model for many years with kids of all ages. A long time ago, during a residency with a group of 7th- and 8th-graders, we "aged up" this activity into a comedy improv-style game, where teaching artists responded to kids' suggestions in the way they would at a comedy club. My co-teaching artist Luke asked the 12- to 14-year-olds for some character suggestions. A kid shouted something. Luke paused, thoughtfully, and said, "I heard pimp . . . I'll shop around." In one breath, Luke validated the kid's contribution, didn't make fun of it, didn't punish him, and yet managed to convey that this is not the kind of suggestion we are likely to use. The kid felt heard, and I didn't have to act like a pimp in front of a bunch of 12-year-olds.

We can translate the design decisions and instructional practices that led Luke to "shop around" into design principles for the learning environments we create. I am using the phrase "learning environments" on purpose. We do teaching and learning a disservice when we limit how we talk about where it happens. Teaching and learning happen in a classroom, for sure. But what about in afterschool and summer programs? Libraries? Museums? Zoos? And don't forget about virtual learning spaces, from online schools to videogames to social media platforms. The people in charge of those learning environments are making active decisions about what people should learn, how they should learn it, how learning is going to be measured, and who counts as a learner in their space.

Design moves us from the *why* of learning to the *how* and *where*. Here, I refer to design as a way of "doing" curriculum, of creating learning experiences that take advantage of what we know people can learn from arts-based experiences and what we know about how good teaching looks. Luke's "shopping around" is an example of working in the moment to create a learning environment that validates creativity and creates constraints for expression. We've already talked about knowing and learning, and you're still reading, so I feel like you're pretty happy with those ideas.[1]

WHY TALK ABOUT DESIGN?

There are a lot of fields that think about and use design as a mechanism for getting work done: architecture, engineering, computer science, the technical arts (costumes, lighting, scenery), to name a few. Designers across all these fields aim to create stuff that people actually use to do something different than they would have done without it. Constructionists call the products of design artifacts. The creators of Fitbit, for example, produce artifacts designed to change people's behaviors. They want people to easily track their exercise, take breaks, move around periodically, and get smarter about how to manage their health. Fitbits are designed for a set of people, for a set of actions, for a set of outcomes. This is the kind of functional design that has meaning to an audience (or a market) that I'm talking about.

In education, we focus on design for intentional learning. *Learning,* meaning you have acquired new skills; created new artifacts, meaning, or relationships; or you are somehow different as a result of having this experience. *Intentional* meaning that, as education designers, we decide what we want people to learn, and then create the conditions for that learning to take place. Intentional is worth mentioning because that is the hardest part of design. Learning, as a natural phenomenon of human interaction, happens around us all the time. As education theorist Etienne Wenger has said: "Learning is something we can assume—whether we see it or not, whether we like the way it goes or not, whether what we are learning is to repeat the past or to shake it off" (1998, p. 9). Stick your hand in a flame and you learn that it hurts and that you shouldn't do that again. Say something inappropriate in a group, someone makes fun of you, and you learn not to speak out in front of that group again. Have a third drink before bed and learn that you are too old to live the life you did before you turned 40.

Many in education would argue that I am talking about curriculum. But it's the design process, and not a curriculum, that we should be focused on. Here's why: Curriculum is an artifact, a fixed entity that is designed by someone else to guide teachers and students through sequenced activities for learning. Once you turn something into a curriculum artifact, it no longer moves, and people have to move around it. Curricular artifacts fueled the ill-fated "what works" movement in education policy—do a bunch of experiments with curriculum (or "interventions," as they are so clinically known), find out which one "works," implement that "at scale," and "Voila!" All children learn all things effectively and efficiently (see Hattie, 2009). When the artifact fails to produce the research-proven results, the conversation shifts to unproductive teacher-blaming: "If the teachers would just implement the curriculum with fidelity, then all of our problems would be solved! We even give them a script, and they can't do that properly. Why are they screwing it all up?" Curriculum designers (even ones who used to be teachers) get to make something, train people to use it, and then wash their hands of the interactions that result. A focus on implementing curricular artifacts with fidelity means that design is something done by other people, not a key feature of the learning process.

Design invites educators and learners to develop the goals and learning processes to support their work. My friend Kurt Squire, one of the world's leading experts on how people learn from videogames, once said that videogames are "designed experiences, resulting from the intersection of design constraints and players' intentions" (2006, p. 26). What he means is that understanding games as designed experiences (rather than as fixed products) acknowledges that players' goals and motivations for playing help determine what they learn from playing as much as what designers intend them to learn. Playing a video game is acting as a co-designer of the learning space. The same is true for any learning experience. Learning is guided by the designers' intentions built into the curricular artifact, and also through how teachers and learners interpret and use the artifacts in terms of their own goals and motivations. The learning process is a continuous co-design that unfolds through interactions between the people and tools involved. If something doesn't work—if learners don't get what you expect them to—there is space to adapt and ways to change up how you work together.

How Do the Arts Matter for Design?

So, why should the arts be the organizing framework for how we design learning environments? Educators have been designing curricula, programs, and schools since formal schooling began, and only a small subset of these approaches are based on the arts. Most take a content-centric approach (Wiggins & McTighe, 2005). A unit about the U.S. Constitution, for example, will be designed around relating information about the core features of the document, the history of how it came to be, and maybe a little about how to do historical inquiry. Content-wise, that's probably fine. But content doesn't begin to get at *how* a group of very different students might struggle with these ideas and how they might demonstrate what they've learned. Most curriculum designers are passionate about the "what" but default to old-school, factory-model stuff—textbooks, worksheets, tests, essays—on the "how."

Emergent, informal learning environments challenge the zeitgeist of desks, textbooks, and exams as core features of schools and open up possibilities for progressive design. Henry Jenkins and his colleagues have described a version of arts-based designed learning environments that they call *participatory cultures*:

A participatory culture is a culture with relatively low barriers to artistic expression and civic engagement, strong support for creating and sharing one's creations, and some type of informal mentorship whereby what is known by the most experienced is passed along to novices. A participatory culture is also one in which members believe their contributions matter, and feel some degree of social connection with one another. (Jenkins et al., 2007, p. 4)

These folks did not begin their studies looking for the arts—they were looking to characterize the informal learning environments that occupy most peoples' learning time. And what they found was artmaking. Artistic expression *is* learning. All design roads lead back to the arts.

What Are Design Principles, and Why Do We Need Them?

"Participatory cultures" is a great *descriptive* term. It tells us what already existing spaces look like and what people do in them. And it tells us that artistic expression is the mode that people default to when they decide to learn on their own. It is not, however, a *prescriptive* term. For those of us who want to create environments that positively impact all kids, we need some prescriptive rules. How do we get from participatory cultures as a descriptive term for the environments where people learn, to creating learning environments for everyone? We need design principles! A review of the field of design-based research describes design principles this way:

Designs evolve from and lead to the development of practical design principles, patterns, and/or grounded theorizing. These principles are not designed to create decontextualized principles or grand theories that function with equal effect in all contexts. Rather, design principles reflect the conditions in which they operate. These tools and conceptual models function to help us understand and adjust both the context and the intervention, so as to maximize learning. (Anderson & Shattuck, 2012, p. 17)

Design principles are the mechanism that lets us communicate what we need in a learning environment for people to get their work done. A design principle of a TV or movie cartoon is that creators use some form of animation. Comic Batman? Cartoon. *Batman* the Animated Series? Cartoon. Adam West in tights? Delightful but not a cartoon. I am not going to give you design principles for making art. Rather, I am going to explain principles for how to redesign all learning environments that draw on core ideas from learning environments where artmaking happens.

THREE THINGS!

One of my all-time favorite warm-up games is called "Three things!" Everyone stands in a circle, and the first person asks the person to their right to name three things from the category of their choice. It can be simple: "Three best ice cream flavors," or, "Three people living or dead you would invite to dinner," or "Three animals you would like to ride." It goes like this:

> *You:* Hey, Erica!
> *Me:* Yes, friend!
> *You:* Give me three animals you would like to ride.
> *Me:* A narwhal!
> *Everyone else:* One!
> *Me:* A mini-horse!
> *Everyone else:* Two!
> *Me:* One of the pigs from Animal Farm!
> *Everyone else:* Three things!

Then, I get to ask the person to my right for three new things. And on and on, until we get around the whole circle. Easy to play, very affirming, and there are no wrong answers. The best kind of game. So, let's imagine these design principles as a game of three things. Here we go!

Design Principle 1: Conceive, Represent, Share

The best way to learn something new is to take an idea or concept, represent it using the tools of a medium, and share it with an audience who has a reason to care about what you're saying. This principle is a more abstract version of the telling, adapting, performing model that has formed the basis of my work with Whoopensocker. In my not-so-humble opinion, all learning environments should be structured around those three core activities: conceive, represent, share. Most of the examples I'll give you here are from my work with kids who create art based on their own life stories, but don't fret! The conceive, represent, share cycle can be applied to everything from a statistics project that highlights injustices in under-resourced neighborhoods (Gutstein, 2006) to incorporating hip-hop cyphers into the science classroom (Adjapong & Emdin, 2015). The conceive, represent, share cycle is universal across subject areas, or at least it ought to be.

I've been talking about this process for a long time—my dissertation work with the About Face Youth Theatre (AFYT) in Chicago gave me a first pass at the design cycle. Back then, I called it, "the dramaturgical process" (Wiley & Feiner, 2001) and focused on the telling, adapting, and performing of narratives of personal experience. When you're telling a story about yourself, something specific happens beyond learning content. Particularly for young people who are struggling to establish a positive sense of self, the translation of tough life stories into pieces of performance art allows them to become more confident, competent learners. During my dissertation work, I followed Maria's story, which became a performance piece that was shared with thousands of audience members at a professional theater in downtown Chicago:

> I let out this big smile and who would have ever thought that that day would be the day that God opened his doors and said, "Maria, I'm introducing you to the person you don't know nor knows who or what she believes in." That day was the day that I was open to a lesbian girl who would teach me about the LGBTQA community. That day I had changed and became who I am now. It's not the entire me, but it's part of me, and I like that.
>
> p.s. This is the day I became happy.

Conceive

In Whoopensocker, we call this part of the process "telling." As a theater artist, I have focused my artmaking and my teaching artist work on the narrative arts. But not all ideas are narrative. Not all art forms are narrative. So, *conceive* is a more inclusive term to describe the first part of the production cycle. What is important to understand is that the first part of creating a successful learning experience is *setting up the conditions for kids to come up with the idea or concept that they want to make their piece about.* I prefer stories, especially stories of personal experiences, but the idea or concept could be anything—Harry Potter, climate change, immigration, the experiences of First Nations peoples; you name it.

So, all we have to do is help kids come up with a great idea. No problem. (Insert wide-eyed emoji here.) Actually, coming up with a good idea is pretty hard. My second BFF besides Tina Fey is Ira Glass, the creator and longtime producer of the radio show *This American Life,* and he is most eloquent on this point:

> One of the things that I think is really hard that nobody ever tells you, if you want to do creative work, is how hard it is to actually find a decent story. . . . But often, and people don't really tell you this, often the amount of time finding the decent story is *more* than the time it takes to produce the story.[2]

So, coming up with good stories or concepts requires a series of designed, iterative activities. I have worked with a lot of groups over the years

whose job it is to get kids to come up with stories, and I have sussed out a
series of must-haves that can be applied directly to the design of a learning
experience (Halverson & Gibbons, 2010):

> **Have an Application Process.** In my work with youth media arts
> organizations, each program asks kids to explain why they want
> to participate in an artmaking process, and describe what story
> they want to tell through writing, an oral interview, or both.
> While some organizations use this method to determine who can
> participate in a program (there is only space for 12 people per
> semester, for example), others have open admissions but still begin
> every production cycle by meeting one-on-one with interested
> participants to have them articulate their initial ideas, and agree
> to see the process through. Unlike school settings, where students
> don't often have to make a pledge to learn, the applications are a
> moment when youth explicitly express their need to tell a story and
> their willingness and dedication to telling it.
>
> **Offer Many Types of Opportunities to Craft Ideas.** I am of the "vote
> early and often" school of idea crafting. (I did come of age in
> Chicago, after all.) In order to get people to find stories, you have
> to provide lots of different ways in. Idea crafting can take the form
> of individual writing time, one-on-one consulting sessions between
> young artists and mentors, group brainstorming discussions, group
> storytelling sessions, "warm-up ideas," where people write or act
> out short pieces, thumbnail sketches, or mini-films. At AFYT, one
> of their go-to idea crafting moves was the story circle. Someone
> tells a story, and then the next person is reminded of a story from
> their own lives that they connect to the first one. The next person
> usually picks up that thematic thread, telling a story that they see
> as connected to the one before (and, possibly, the one before that).
> What emerges is a story chain, connected by similar ideas and
> structures that the storytellers see as relevant across their stories.
> Often, people get ideas for topics that emerge from their story
> chain—some examples of that at AFYT included stories about
> acts of queer identity disclosure and how AIDS affected different
> socioeconomic and racial communities (Halverson, 2010b).
> These story chain topics are both personal to the tellers and offer
> opportunities for educators to connect to academic content, for
> example AIDS as a public health crisis.
>
> **Be Flexible on "Whose Idea" It Is.** It is important to open up the
> possibility that ideas might belong to more than one person. I've
> already described how artmaking supports both individualist and
> collectivist identity processes and outcomes. In arts practice, it is
> common for an individual young artist to produce a solo piece

of work from their personal story or passion-project idea. But I have also seen young artists find a group of people to work with after pitching their story ideas, and then work together to develop an idea that was relevant for them and their broader community. Most of the truly collaborative artmaking I've witnessed has been in communities that take a more collective perspective on identity. Being open to multiple kinds of idea authorship means that not only can we value collaboration as an outcome, but we can greatly increase our chances that learning will happen for everyone in the room.

It is essential that learners have a clear idea before beginning any production process. Wherever I have studied youth artmaking, young artists who never quite clarified what story they wanted to tell, or what idea they wanted to pursue, either never completed their projects, or relied heavily on artist-mentors to help them finish. From a design perspective, scaffolding the idea generation and refinement process in a way that makes sense for the community in which the work is taking place encourages all participants to become successful producers rather than rely on personal vision or passion.

Represent

So, you've gotten everyone to come up with strong ideas, and they're excited to start making! Now, what do you do? Well, artmaking is an act of translating ideas into media for sharing, what we call "adapting" in Whoopensocker-speak. The job of artists is to express the core ideas of their stories using the tools of the artistic medium in which they are working. Remember, representation is the single most important act both in making art and in learning. Creating, critiquing and sharing representations are the primary means to learning, and the arts are the best way to participate in representation. We already know that. What we have not yet explored is how educators can *design for other people* to create representations. To do so, you have to set learners up to understand (1) what kinds of tools are available in that medium, and (2) how those tools communicate meaning effectively.

Macrolevel Tools. Let's start with a macrolevel decision: picking a genre. Genres provide a collection of resources and patterns that constrain what people can make and how tools get used to engage in a certain kind of production. Everything from Chicano Art Movement–style screen printing, to a puppet show, to a podcast in the style of *This American Life* counts as a genre. By using a genre to define, in advance, the ways tools can fit together, artmakers pay attention to what combination allows them to best represent their ideas. Folks who've been making art for a long time can choose their own genre—that can also be part of the design process. But for newcomers, it is essential that we pre-select a genre to provide constraints to inform a pathway for representation.

One of my favorite genres to work with is the *This American Life* radio story. I love this genre for several reasons. First, audio production of this kind of narrative constrains the number of tools available to producers. Making a movie (especially if you've never made one before) is overwhelming. Making an audio story is less so: All you have is sound. Second, *This American Life* offers a structure that newcomers can easily latch onto—each episode is comprised of acts (like a play) of similar lengths, and is tied together by a shared theme. Finally, there are *tons* of examples (over 700, by the publishing of this book—free audio archive is available at: www. thisamericanlife.org/archive). This means that your learners can start by listening, analyzing, and talking about what this genre contains—something I also build into my designed environments.

Microlevel Tools. In *This American Life,* microlevel tools include dialogue, soundtrack, tone, and timbre, and choices about how those tools interact. A fancy word for tools here is *mode*, as in the mode used for expression. Artistic expression is *multimodal*, meaning it simultaneously contains multiple modes. If you want to get really fancy, we can talk about the meaning that is made when different modes interact: the kineikonic mode (Burn & Parker, 2003). Imagine a little animated heart; it's red with a black outline, and it's pulsing on a white background. Now, imagine Edvard Grieg's "Morning Mood" playing in background. That heart probably looks serene and sweet, possibly a representation of love. The song switches and "Metal Health (Bang Your Head)" by Quiet Riot is playing. How does the heart look now? I'm imagining that it's pulsing, because it's been stomped on or thrown away. The meaning that you make of that heart drawing with each of those pieces of music is the kineikonic mode. Artmakers should be able to identify the multiple modes they can work with *and* how those modes interact to make meaning.

So, let's talk through an example, using a film you're already familiar with: *The Mizz Perception of Roro!* Quick reminder from Chapter 3, this is an autobiographical short film about a young African American woman trying to tackle misperceptions about tall women. Consider her use of cinematography as a microtool to create an extreme visual perspective. She uses a top-down angle to give the feeling of being Roro and a bottom-up angle to give the feeling of being seen by Roro. When she layers sound on top, Roro's voiceover adds meaning to her visual choices. She first asks, "Why do people view me like that or . . . you know what I'm sayin'? What goes through people's minds when they see me?" This question is in direct response to the prior scene, where an interviewee tells Roro that people think she is "mean" and "tough" when they first meet her. The first person, bird's-eye view shot gives the impression that Roro is much bigger than the person in the frame, providing evidence that her size may be intimidating to others. When we consider the mise-en-scéne, that is, what is inside the frame, Roro's wave to the camera in the second upward-tilt shot provides a direct counterpoint both to the interviewees' descriptions of her as mean and tough and to the bird's-eye view shot that makes her appear visually intimidating. Whew! So much packed into a 10-second film clip. And *lots* of metarepresentational competence involved.

Share

Now, for the fun part: sharing. Sharing representations is an inextricable part of the artmaking process; it is not an extra step to take only if there is time. We have to design for sharing in the same way we design for conceiving and for representing. In sharing-as-design, it matters that we think about (1) how the work will be shared, (2) with whom, and (3) in what context. That is because the audience is a hugely important component of artmaking. That makes sense, practically; if you've ever made anything, you seldom realize the power of what you've created until someone else sees it. Added bonus: This also makes sense theoretically. Alecia Magnifico writes about how young people become good writers, both through formal schooling and by taking part in participatory cultures. She shows how "audience" is a bridging concept between the different ways we understand what good writing looks like. Audiences who choose to engage with the work can provide the kinds of suggestions makers can use for real improvement. Whether you believe learning is primarily a cognitive process (something that happens in your head), or a sociocultural process (something that happens in the world across people, tools, and time), "audience" is there. We either imagine an audience when we make decisions about how to write, or we see learning as only possible when an audience consumes our writing. Or it's both. The point is Alecia's work provides the *theoretical justification* for why sharing with an audience is a necessary part of the design of learning experiences (Magnifico, 2010).

But we're not just talking about any old audience. We need an *authentic* audience. A classroom teacher is an audience; so is a parent. However, if the teacher is not seen as a legitimate, expert practitioner, or as someone who genuinely cares about the work, sharing will not be the transformative act that it can be for students. Kids performing stories in a classroom are more eager to hear the opinions of their Whoopensocker teaching artists, whom they have seen both in the classroom and onstage. My daughter became much more interested in what her biology teacher had to say about her ideas when she found out they spent several years in South America identifying birds before becoming a teacher. Young artists are much more willing to spend time making difficult representational decisions when they know that those who will be viewing their work are people who have real expertise with concepts and tools.

Now, I know what you're thinking: "But can't I just make something for myself? Why does everything I make have to be shared with someone else? Stop putting so much pressure on me!" I am not a monster. You can make all the art you want and never share it with anyone, and have it be a fully satisfying experience. But when we're talking about designing learning experiences—meaning we are invested in people getting something out of participating in a learning experience—sharing work with an authentic audience is a must. An audience can provide real feedback that affords authentic assessment. I will talk more in the next section about assessment (a bad word in many progressive learning communities, but a positive force for learning in the arts); here, it's important to mention that you can't collect feedback without an audience. And, feedback, as Julian Sefton-Green would say, is everything: "The feedback from the experience of public production is crucial for all forms of cultural production" (2000), and this feedback is crucial for evaluating student work.

Another big reason learners need authentic audiences is that they allow educators (classroom teachers, mentors, teaching artists, whoever!) to shift their role from judge to ally. When the educator is the arbiter of quality, it is much harder for young artmakers to work *with* that educator rather than *for* them. You are a student. Or you have been one. How many times have you thought, "I just wish I knew what the teacher wanted, then I could just do it, and be done." We're going for the opposite, here. The educator is there to say things like, "Who do you imagine will see this work? What do you want them to take from it? What do we have to do to get this piece ready for them to see it?" This perspective is way more motivating and offers a chance for educators and artmakers to forge productive relationships. I see this in all of the creative production environments I teach in, no matter the age of the learners and no matter the kind of work artists are creating.

While the concept of audience—and authentic audience, in particular—is an obvious component of artmaking, the good news is that this idea works for other school subjects too. Take the example of a math project that asks students to redesign local play spaces and present their plans to city councils and other decision-making bodies. Redesigning a playground for your teacher to "check the math?" Meh. Redesigning a playground so that your hometown might build something that you and your friends actually want to use? Aces (Turner et al., 2009).

Design Principle 2: Assessment: Authentic, Embedded, and Constant

We can't talk about the design of learning environments without coming around to assessment. For educators of all kinds—from teachers to parents to librarians to artists—the question of how we know what people have learned is usually at the top of our minds. I am here to take assessment back from the clutches of evaluators, graders, and rankers, and, instead, help you think about why and how it is part of designing a good arts-based curriculum.

One of the beautiful features of artmaking is that assessment is naturally embedded in both the process and product. We don't have to *create* authentic assessment opportunities; we just have to take advantage of the ones that are there. Assessment is an integral part of the production cycle and includes both formative (ongoing) and summative (final) components. There are two ways that we can think about what learners get out of their participation in a learning environment: assessment of process and assessment of product. In other words, we can think of assessment both in terms of what is happening as people are making and what they made as a result of that process.

Assessment of the Process. There are several existing structures for thinking about how to assess the artmaking processes. Probably the most well-known is *critique*, made famous in art schools and salons around the world. Critique provides a great foundation for looking at the process of learning and for supporting peoples' engagement with the representational trajectory—not just to make art but to make anything. Critique is baked into the representational trajectory; participating in critique builds vocabulary and generates a shared set of language practices among artists. But critique is also a form of assessment (Soep, 2006). The purpose of critique is not only to improve students' products but to reflect on the decisions they make in the moment and to improve the processes they use to make those decisions. Reflection and improvement conversations are often led by teachers; this is common in studio-art classes in high schools and in colleges (Hetland et al., 2013; Sawyer, 2018). In youth arts programs, critique is often cofacilitated by the young people themselves (Soep, 2006).

Keith Sawyer describes critiques as laying bare mismatches between what the artists think they have done and how their work is received. How others react to the work provides evidence that what the artist thinks they have represented and what is being "read" are two different things (Sawyer, 2018). Studio Thinking scholars summarize critiques this way: "Critiques have two distinguishing features that earn them a place of honor in the studio classroom. First, they focus attention on students' work and working processes. And, second, critiques are explicitly social" (Hetland et al., 2013, p. 26). These features of critique are true, whether you are throwing a pot or creating a performance piece about the time your brother told your sister he was "eating poops," but, really, he was eating chocolate chips, and then she demanded poops from your mom. (A Whoopensocker classic, you'll get the whole story in the final chapter as a reward for making it to the end.)

But what does a social, working critique process actually look like? The first, most important step is what I call, getting beyond "good job!" People like to hear that they've done a good job, but it doesn't tell them how to make their work better, or even highlight how people are responding to their work. The best resource for getting artmakers to engage in critique is through what the fine people at Harvard Project Zero call "thinking routines" (pz.harvard.edu/thinking-routines). These are practical suggestions for how to have conversations with people around work and work processes. They even have a section called "thinking with art and objects," which has some of my favorites, including the classic "See, Think, Wonder." I have adapted this routine to help groups respond to their peers' works in progress, by answering the following questions:

- What do you notice?
- What does this remind you of?
- How does it make you feel?
- What do you want to know more about?

These forms of critique give artmakers substantive responses to their work, while avoiding the dreaded "I like . . . ," or, "I don't like . . . ," and the even less helpful (though much more friendly) "good job!"

Another place I have looked for help with *how* to engage in the assessment of process is in a small town in Italy, Reggio Emilia.[3] The Reggio Emilia approach, most common in early childhood, focuses on kids' arts inquiries as the foundation for all learning (Edwards et al., 1991). The approach includes a process they call *documentation,* a method of valuing not just what kids make, but the process they use to make it and how they understand what they're making. It's important that we do not confuse documentation with display. We all hang our kids' pictures on the refrigerator, and post performances on Facebook. Classrooms are filled with children's responses to art prompts. But documentation is so much more. Much like thinking routines, documentation can make thinking visible as part of assessment rather than the precursor to assessment. A documentation includes a product, but it also contains the artmaker's reflections on what they made, descriptions of how they came to be interested in what they made, and a representation of the process they engaged in to make it. With very young children (most Reggio Emilia schools are preschools), the teacher serves as the documenter. In learning environments with older students, the students themselves are responsible for both what they make and their documentation of the process.

Some of these practices are already in use in many schools and learning environments. Portfolios of work for end-of-the-year assessments is a great start. These portfolios can include design journals, sketches, attempts at problem solving, works in progress—any artifacts that were generated as part of production. The analysis I shared of Frank's graphic-design piece included all of these artifacts. Tiff Tseng (2016) calls this form of process-oriented documentation "make-throughs." A make-through is a form of documentation that allows producers to both capture their process as they develop a project and to showcase the iterations of their project in community with others. Make-throughs allow learners to capture, share, reflect, and situate their learning as natural extensions of the production process.

Assessment of Product. The cool thing about making art is that, when you're done, you have made *something* you can point to, and say, "I did that!" Artifacts capture conceiving, representing, and sharing so it's only natural that we would want to do something with that artifact. There is a longstanding tension between those who want to reduce production to its technical components and those who want to romanticize creativity to the point where any critical impulse is read as impinging on a young person's inherent capacity to express themselves (Sefton-Green, 2000). I say "phooey" to that tension! This is a false dichotomy; we can both rely on external audience appreciation of quality *and* develop a set of internal technical measures that everyone is happy with. Yes, and . . . !

You might be nervous about relying on audiences: What if they don't come? What if they are hostile or unwilling to provide feedback? *What if you need to assign grades?* Alright, alright, I can hear you; you don't have to shout. First, you can (and must!) design your audience is well. In a project where we worked with 5th-graders and their teachers to make puppets using sewable circuitry and then create puppet shows about environmental issues, we invited audiences of kindergartners to attend the puppet shows (Litts et al., 2020). The artists used their audience as a design feature, around which they made decisions about their puppetry. Knowing that younger kids would be the audience for their puppet shows, they actively leveraged what they knew about kindergarten literacies to produce work and they got direct feedback on whether they had "gotten it right" from the questions, laughter, and applause from their kindergarten audience. Adult panels of experts work well as audiences, too. Bringing playground designs to the city council and hearing their feedback is an excellent way to evaluate math, engineering, and architectural knowledge and skills. And students are much more likely to take critique from people who actually "do" the work than they are from the teacher who has guided them through the process.

You can also develop an internal set of criteria for looking at the artifacts; in teacher world, they're called rubrics. Rubrics allow designers to set up categories of quality and to specify the levels of performance within each rubric domain. I won't reinvent the wheel here, but I will point you to some work by Jessie Nixon and her teacher-collaborators who studied how to do assessment in high school film classes. One mechanism they developed was having high school students create a producer's commentary for surfacing metarepresentational competence. The rubric allowed teachers to understand how students articulated the relationship between the idea they intended to represent and the tools they used through students' verbal commentary overlayed on top of the film (Nixon, 2020). While this idea is specific to filmmaking, allowing students to tell you what they have learned through the products they create is not.

Design Principle 3: Ideas First, Tools Second

It is pretty common in schools to require people to learn "the basics" before they can move on to the fun stuff. Want to be an engineer and design new tools to alleviate climate change? Better learn all your math equations first! Want to design a videogame where unicorns fight dragons? Better learn Python, or Unity, or *at least* HTML. There are many problems with this plan. First, people often abandon ship before they get to do anything cool. Second, it doesn't reflect the way people learn to do things in the wild. Third, tools are constantly changing. (Okay, maybe math equations aren't changing, but how you calculate answers is. Have you seen your kid's graphing calculator? Sheesh.) Designing through the arts calls for a "just in time" approach to tools that says "ideas first, tools second."

The foundational text for the study of videogames and learning—*What Videogames Have to Teach Us About Literacy and Learning*—outlines 36(!) learning principles taken from videogames that can help reorganize formal learning environments (Gee, 2007). While they are all valuable, for this conversation, I refer you to Principle 27: "Explicit Information On-Demand and Just-In-Time Principle: Information is provided at crucial times to maximize proper responses."

This means that good videogames give players access to information exactly when they need it. It keeps players interested, doesn't bombard them with unnecessary details, and allows them to make seamless progress. Similarly, the artmaking spaces that I have created and studied rest on the idea that people will learn to use the tools that are appropriate to the task they need to accomplish within the conceive, represent, and share cycle. No person's process is completely idiosyncratic. Youth are constantly working with peers, instructors, and artist-mentors to share knowledge about the skills and tools necessary to improve their making. Instructors often provide lessons on specific techniques to the whole group that they know from experience youth will need at certain times in the creative process. For example, one of the youth media arts organizations I studied gave formal lessons on the documentary interviewing process, from options for shooting video footage to the development of interview questions to examining the relationship between the filmmaker and their interviewees. Other times, group lessons or one-on-one mentoring sessions were spontaneous, based on the needs of participants that arose. These are not predesigned lessons, nor are they predictable in advance of the process. The excerpt I shared in Chapter

4 of Breana learning from her mentors while editing an interview clip of her grandma exemplifies these one-on-one sessions. In both whole-group and one-on-one instruction, students' needs dictate what is taught, and not the other way around.

FROM CURRICULUM TO DESIGN

I am making two, interrelated arguments about how the arts can transform the way we design curriculum as the mechanism for changing instruction. First, arts practices should serve as the foundation for how we design all of our learning environments. We should engage learners in cycles of conceiving, representing, and sharing all the time. We should assess learning early and often through practices like critique and documentation, and we should lean into what students want to learn by offering just-in-time lessons on particular skills or tools as they're needed. Second, and equally important, instruction should be more like design than like implementation of curriculum. I want teachers to think like chefs, not cooks. Following a recipe almost always ends up with the food tasting *not quite* as good as it would if it was made by the person who wrote the recipe. Chefs understand why the ingredients are in the recipe and can adapt the ingredients to suit the needs of diners. Good instruction is about thinking like a designer in a space where curricula provide a rich set of resources for customizing learning to the needs and interests of learners. Nick was successful in Whoopensocker because the experience designed around him supported what he brought to the classroom and allowed for the kind of adaptations he needed. Lamar could step into his role as a knight because the design afforded him space to do so. And sometimes, as a teaching artist, you need the authority and the skills to shop around.

CHAPTER 6

The Arts Take Center Stage

By now, you are probably thinking, "This is so great, there must be a Whoopensocker-like program in every school! All schools must give kids the opportunity to conceive, represent, and share their ideas." And while I would love to say that every Maria, Nick, and Lamar have had the designed experiences I just described, as of 2015, less than 5% of public elementary schools offered formal classes in dance and theater (Bowen & Kisida, 2017). The picture is a little less bleak when it comes to the visual arts and music, but we are all familiar with the language of "specials" or "electives" to describe the arts in school. Despite our best efforts to share the life-changing impacts on kids, the arts remain in the margins.

Reframing learning, teaching, and the design of learning environments in the way that I am advocating will not just happen automatically. Or even with a little bit of work. It starts by valuing artmaking as intrinsic to education and ends with the arts taking center stage. This requires a whole new vision for schooling, like the one Elliot Eisner described in his final, posthumously published essay:

> It is an educational culture that has a greater focus on becoming than being, places more value on the imaginative than on the factual, assigns greater priority to valuing than measuring, and regards the quality of the journey as more educationally significant than the speed at which the destination is reached. I am talking about a new vision of what education might become and what schools are for. (Eisner, 2004, p. 10)

Arts practices show us how we transform learning, teaching, and design to improve our education systems. I am not alone in this belief. In advocating for the crucial role that the arts play in teaching and learning, researchers at the Neuro-Education Initiative (NEI) at Johns Hopkins University make this bold statement: "The arts should no longer be viewed as the *victim* of public policy but instead become the *driver* of reform" (Hardiman & John Bull 2019, p. 8, emphasis in original). While there is an arts integration movement in U.S. schools (Burnaford et al., 2007) and large-scale research studies, like those conducted at NEI, demonstrate that school-based participation in arts programs positively impact students' academic and social and emotional learning (see also Bowen & Kisida, 2019), there has not yet been any large-scale national investment in school-based arts practices to drive education reform.

So, why hasn't this happened? Since 2000, ambitious reforms that focus on literacy, math, and science learning have sidelined the arts as a valuable pathway to learning. Arts advocates get caught up in a vicious cycle of justifying how the arts can be used to address persistent achievement problems in education, which are assessed only by standardized measures like test scores and grades. When swallowed up by those efforts, we lose the intrinsic value that the arts can bring to revitalize teaching and learning in the first place. But there is new hope! STEAM—science, technology, engineering, arts, and mathematics—as well as the Maker Movement, offer potential mechanisms for fully realizing the potential of arts practices in education (Mejias et al., 2021). STEAM and making go beyond using the arts in service of traditional disciplines and instead identify the shared practices that transform all learning. But before we talk about how STEAM and making can serve as the bridge into a new vision for our education system, we need to know how we got here.

ACT I: THE ACCOUNTABILITY MACHINE

There is always a tension between the *liberal goals* for arts education (which include self-expression, feeling, engagement, creativity, and ownership) and *utilitarian goals* (which focus on form, technique, and experience). This tension has dominated our conversations about the value of the arts in education in Western contexts throughout modern schooling (Fleming et al., 2015). The recent national bias toward utilitarian goals shows how the arts have struggled to secure their place at the forefront of discussions about improving teaching, learning, and design. Efforts to place the arts at the center of education reform conversations have been particularly challenged by the accountability movement, made famous by the 1983 report, "A Nation at Risk" (Eisner, 2002). The report hit the panic button on the "rising tide of mediocrity" emerging in American schools and called for an intense examination of curriculum and instructional strategies to focus on utilitarian basic skills to ensure American schools were *the best* and our kids *the most prepared* (Hardiman & John Bull, 2019). The rhetoric of collective panic continued with phrases like the 2002 "No Child Left Behind" legislation and the 2009 "Race to the Top" initiative that rewarded states and school districts that could show improvement on standardized exams in math and literacy learning. As an arts educator, I had a lot of questions about this framing. Why is this a race? Why are we competing against one another? How do we know when we've reached "the top"? And, most importantly, why are we obsessed with math and literacy scores as the criteria for success?

I have seen, through my college teaching, what happens when the best and brightest race to institutions of higher education in large numbers and with great speed via the standardized testing expressway. These learners seem to lack some qualities that I have found are essential for productive learning and happy living. Joy. Excitement. Openness. Capacity for risk-taking. Interest in critique. The arts provide opportunities for the development of these qualities. But, as Fleming and his colleagues note: "There has been understandable reluctance to emphasise notions of joy and entertainment for fear of reducing the status of the arts in educational contexts" (2015, p. 4). We shouldn't hide these features under a bushel; instead, we ought to be desperate to bring arts-based ways of knowing, doing, and being into our classrooms. But I am getting ahead of myself. Let me take you back, *Wayne's World*–style, to the year 2000.

The emergence of international comparisons among students for test score performance built a fear-mongering narrative that American students were "behind other kids" around the world in the race to be the best (National Commission on Excellence in Education, 1983). This depiction of "A Nation at Risk" focused conversations at the policy and practice level around a narrowed curriculum, a set of subjects that were (1) measurable, (2) aligned with international measures, and (3) could be tested within the context of the school day (Hardiman & John Bull, 2019). This discussion also narrowed the purpose of schooling. Mainstream education left behind John Dewey's ideas of the role of project-based, student-initiated learning (Dewey, 1938) and Paulo Freire's ideas about education as raising student consciousness in order to change the system (Freire & Macedo, 1987) in favor of efficient, research-proven measures to raise scores.

The hyperfocus on kids' reading and math test scores reached a fever pitch in the 2002 *No Child Left Behind Act* (commonly known by its acronym, NCLB). The law aimed to address the basic inequalities in American classrooms by holding all schools accountable to test-based performance measures. During the 1990s, policymakers, educators, and researchers collaborated to develop content standards for math and literacy in K–12 education. NCLB took standardization to the next level by requiring states to develop tests that would measure how all learners performed in terms of the content standards. It also required states to make test-score results (as well as local school demographic information) public to create community awareness of how their schools were improving test score performance. Aggregated school-level scores for math and literacy became, seemingly overnight, the universally accepted index of both school quality and student learning. The grades schools received for student test score performance became how we judged the quality of education. Achievement over inquiry, indeed.

There have been critiques of this reductionism out the wazoo throughout the NCLB era. Leading scholars on issues of race and education have spoken loudly about the ways that the law forces school districts and states to compete with one another—for teachers, for funding, and, ultimately, for students—which has the adverse effect of leaving the same children even more behind than before, specifically Black and Brown students, English learners, and students with special-education designations (Darling-Hammond, 2007; Leonardo, 2007). At the curricular level, focusing exclusively on what will be tested on standardized measures of reading and math reduces the range of what kinds of curricula dominate schooling and ends up turning teaching into testing (Gay, 2007). NCLB set up an *accountability machine* based on test performance as a way to measure the quality of teachers, schools, and students, and encouraged educators to reduce good teaching, learning, and curriculum to narrow, standardized ways of knowing, doing, and being (Au, 2011). The reduction of education to math and literacy test performance left very little room for the arts. As struggling schools received increased pressure to improve test scores, frantic educators allocated more and more time to math and reading instruction. This intense focus on measuring math and reading scores left "untested" or "untestable" subjects like the arts out in the cold (Mishook & Kornhaber, 2006). At least domains like social studies and science could be enlisted into efforts to improve disciplinary reading skill improvement (Marx & Harris, 2006; Pace, 2011).

So, how did arts educators and researchers respond to this national narrowing process? We did what artists have always done: We adapted. One productive adaptation was to demonstrate that artmaking improves math and literacy outcomes. An "if you can't beat 'em, join 'em" kind of strategy, that Eisner calls, "using the arts to promote academic performance" (2002, p. 38). Arts education researchers made some progress with this instrumentalizing approach, documenting a range of causal links between a specific artmaking activity and gains on core skills in reading and math. A "Critical Links" compendium was collected for the Department of Education, offering connections between individual arts programs and academic or socioemotional learning outcomes (Arts Education Partnership, 2002). Arts and education researcher James Catterall provided his take on these studies:

> Research on the arts and learning has far transcended the need to test whether or not the arts have impacts with potential manifestations beyond direct learning in the art forms. Of present interest is just what are such manifestations and what can be said of their importance or how they come about. (p. 154)

As you might imagine, this statement alone was not enough to move the accountability machine with respect to the arts. What are these manifestations? And how do they have impacts? It turns out that the "potential manifestations" are fairly modest. In synthesizing all of the studies on the transfer of learning from the arts to core, academic subjects, Hetland and Winner (2004) found the following:

- Learning music has some connections to improvements in mathematical spatial reasoning.
- Engaging in classroom-based drama activities can improve outcomes on verbal and written portions of reading exams.
- The verbal and quantitative SAT scores are slightly higher for high school students who take arts classes.

Unfortunately, insisting on adapting arts-based programs to improve math and literacy outcomes is a little like forcing educators to use a wheelbarrow when they already own a car. You can improve math and literacy outcomes, incidentally, through the arts, but if your goal is to pass the test, why not just use a research-proven curriculum designed for passing tests? It is not compelling to tell teachers and administrators who are under pressure to perform that they should take the arts wheelbarrow instead of the faster, more efficient, test-prep car.

Acquiescence is an adaptation, but so is resistance. Even as Hetland and Winner outlined the ways in which the arts could serve an instrumentalized function in schooling, they concluded their argument with this clear statement:

> Perhaps the most important policy implications of the research reported here is that arts education policy should not be based on instrumental outcomes for the arts, whether or not these outcomes can be demonstrated. If they cannot be demonstrated, the case is clear: We must make honest arguments for the importance of the arts. But even in cases where they can be demonstrated, we should not use instrumental outcomes as justifications. (2004, pp. 157–158)

They argued for a shift in focus, away from the instrumental argument, toward what the arts-as-subjects can give to learners. The arts needs research that examines the outcomes of arts education in and of itself as well as what other school subjects can learn about good teaching and learning.

ACT II: THE RISE OF STEM

It is not only the arts that suffered as a result of the accountability machine. Anything that could not be transformed into a vehicle for improving reading and math test scores—biology, computer science, geography, history, physical education—was left out of the education reform conversation. Enter STEM, the nearly ubiquitous acronym in education circles that represents science, technology, engineering, and mathematics. The National Science Foundation popularized the STEM phrase in the 2000s,[1] primarily as a way to characterize collective disciplinary skills and practices needed to build a successful, competitive technology workforce. Charles Vela, founder of the

Center for Advancement of Hispanics in Science and Engineering Education, is credited with first promoting the STEM acronym in order to both advance the idea and to make those who had been historically underrepresented in STEM fields a priority in education policy (Gonzalez & Kuenzi, 2012). While STEM isn't used exclusively to describe education, its primary function is to solidify what disciplinary expertise students need in order to make the U.S. globally competitive in the science and technology enterprise. As a result, education reform efforts were able to argue STEM's importance in the education hierarchy, elevating its status in schools (Mejias et al., 2021). In 2007, The National Academies of Science, Engineering, and Medicine produced a report with the alarmist-sounding title, "Rising Above the Gathering Storm: Energizing and Employing America for a Brighter Economic Future." Reports like this helped to push STEM to the forefront of our K–12 schooling priorities (Hardiman & John Bull, 2019).

By 2012, the federal government was investing $3 billion per year in STEM education initiatives with about one-third of this money going to K–12 (Gonzalez & Kuenzi, 2012). While these efforts yielded improvements in academic achievement and interest in preparation for STEM-related college and careers, the persistent achievement gap between historically underrepresented populations of students and male, White, and Asian students did not narrow at all. Later in the 2010s, many scholars and education leaders began to focus their efforts on building new approaches to include underrepresented students and communities of color into a new, more equitable STEM pipeline (Mejias et al., 2021). However, paying attention to pathways to a revitalized workforce have continued to privilege disciplinary knowledge in science, math, and technology as high-priority areas of national education focus.

Scene i: It's not STEM, It's STEAM!

The rise of STEM has provided a fruitful context for arts educators and researchers to re-insert the arts into conversations about what counts in education. Putting the "A" in STEM, or STEAM, has allowed the arts to rise to the top. (I'm sure this joke has been made 1,000 times, but I couldn't resist. Sorry not sorry.) Advocates began by arguing for integrating the arts into STEM as a mechanism for introducing creativity and broadening participation in science, technology, engineering, and mathematics. And there is evidence that the arts make STEM teaching and learning better, specifically around creativity, innovation, and problem-solving (Stewart et al., 2019).

These initial arguments for STEAM looked more like the instrumental case for the arts in NCLB (Mejias et al., 2021). Since then, STEAM has opened the door for a more substantive conversation about the relationship between STEM and the arts. Sam Mejias and colleagues argue that we should aim for a "mutually instrumental" relationship between the arts and STEM, where "all disciplines [are] equal and in dialogic conversation, making the motivation for STEAM one based on interdisciplinarity" (2021, p. 218). Further, they describe the importance of focusing on pedagogy in order to also value theories of teaching and learning that both come from STEAM and can inform STEAM activities. The STEAM framework can allow the pedagogical features of the arts to take center stage:

> Art-science programs have demonstrated the strong effects that such approaches can have on learners—removing them from specific identities of the "artsy" or "mathsy" person and placing them in a context that is purpose driven, offering an opportunity for creative and flexible thinking that maps onto their key outcomes. (Bevan et al., 2019, p. 25)

There are some outstanding examples of projects that embrace an art-science perspective, putting all the letters in STEAM on the same plane. At Tech Tales, families build dioramas using robotics, connecting artmaking, computer programming, and robotics through Indigenous stories of culture, history, and society (Tzou et al., 2019). The Digital Youth Divas program engages middle-school girls from nondominant communities in e-textile and programming activities, using narrative storytelling (Pinkard et al., 2017). UK-based botanist Anne Osbourn built the Science, Art, and Writing Initiative as a way to use science to inspire visual art and creative writing. And through the use of scientific images to prompt creative artmaking, kids understand and express complex scientific ideas, including how bacteria function and how infectious diseases spread (Osbourn, 2019).

This framing of STEAM as mutually instrumental and pedagogical is promising and exciting. We need more examples like these. The only caution I would offer is to avoid what I call the "put a bird on it" phenomenon. This meme is derived from the sketch TV show *Portlandia*, which focused on life in hipster Portland, Oregon. The phrase describes, literally, putting the image of a bird on something, typically "handcrafted" or "thrifted," which then makes the item "more artistic." Imagine a sticker for your laptop, a patch for your denim jacket, or a hand-stitched detail you added to a skirt you bought at a thrift store.[2] In STEAM education, putting a bird on it looks like decorating your science project or coloring in your answers on a math worksheet. It could even look like writing and performing a play on cell mitosis, if the only thing that anyone *really* cares about is whether kids know the phases of mitosis. A lot of us have birds on our stuff. And people like birds. The issue is not the birds. It's that it has become shorthand, an easy way to check the creativity box and move on. When we put a little token "a" in STEM, we don't really get to STEAM.

As we know from research on science knowledge in Indigenous communities, it is all too easy for STEM learning environments to minimize other ways of knowing and doing as unscientific and, therefore, less valuable (Barajás-Lopez & Bang, 2018). It is especially easy for the arts to be relegated to the treat kids get for participating, or the consolation prize for kids who are seen as struggling with regular STEM. So, while we may engage a few more kids, putting a bird on it does not change our values in any way around what counts as good teaching, learning, or design. The way to avoid putting a bird on it is through what Bronwyn Bevan and colleagues (2019) call "epistemic intersections"—ways of knowing, doing, and being that stretch across both STEM and the arts. The intersections happen in three sets of practices that promote learning, especially for those who have historically been marginalized from mainstream institutions: exploration, meaning-making, and critiquing. These three practices share many similarities with the ways I have characterized learning and design in and through the arts: developing ideas, creating representations to share insights, and engaging interested audiences to critique and refine work.

Scene ii: STEAM Meets the Maker Movement

A specific route into the STEM pipeline has come along in the form of the Maker Movement. Around the time that people started putting the "a" in STEM, making became popularized in education circles. Through federal policy office hubs like the Office of Science and Technology Policy, and through do-it-yourself movements around the world, the Maker Movement has aimed to change our collective values around teaching and learning from the bottom up. The maker movement refers broadly to the growing number of people who are engaged in the creative production of artifacts in their daily lives and who find physical and digital forums to share the processes and products with others (Halverson & Sheridan, 2014) and is inclusive of analog and digital practices such as woodworking, soldering, cooking, programming, painting, and crafting (Halverson & Peppler, 2018). The Maker Movement includes, (1) *makerspaces*—informal sites where communities come together to create, (2) *maker activities*—projects that embrace STEAM learning found everywhere from classrooms to homes across the world, and (3) *maker faires*—large-scale events that operate like a science fair and a Renaissance faire made a beautiful STEAM baby. Federal initiatives, beginning with a White House Maker Faire in 2014, signaled a commitment to STEM education through a more playful, creative, and entrepreneurial lens. President Obama's embrace of the DIY culture that characterized an explosion of interest in making as an alternative to formal STEM education opened up possibilities for creative, cultural, artistic, and "homegrown" processes and practices that have made their way into the formal and, sometimes, conservative world of STEM education.

Nowadays, we can find making in informal learning settings, including libraries, museums, independent makerspaces, and after-school programs.

Schools have also participated in the Maker Movement through the establishment of school-based makerspaces and by incorporating maker activities into everyday classroom practices (Halverson & Peppler, 2018). Making comes in from the side, not through the established disciplinary practices of school-based STEM learning. As a result, the goals and outcomes of participation in maker-based learning can be more open-ended than goals set through STEM disciplines. A focus on processes like tinkering, playing, and designing means that making is not beholden to math standards or requirements for students to enter college science or engineering classes. Making, Sam Mejias and colleagues argue, "can provide new pathways for underrepresented and historically marginalized communities to recognize and engage with the implications of these historical and structural legacies" (2021, p. 226).

Making has the potential to democratize STEM and to build some of the mutuality with the arts that STEAM aims for. More, different people have access to tools and skills that were previously only available to experts. With a 3D printer, for example, everyone can produce their own gadgets and solve their own problems. I have seen large-scale creations at maker faires, such as 50-foot Rube Goldberg machines, a scale-model recreation of the Taj Mahal made of popsicle sticks, and a metal dragon that breathes fire. I have also seen small creations make inventor culture more available to solve everyday problems—like an automatic dog feeder for when you can't be home all day with your dog. The outside interests people bring into the formal STEM world become part of what counts as valuable, bridging gaps between what schools want people to learn and what people actually want to know and do.

In summer 2013, the Children's Museum of Pittsburgh invited local-area makers to submit their projects to share with a public audience. One of the projects at the museum's maker faire, made by two self-identified Orthodox Jewish men, featured a mezuzah that would talk and sing, as a person crossed the threshold of the doorway. Maybe you're thinking, "What's a mezuzah?" You are not alone. Most of the maker faire's visitors did not know what a mezuzah was, and the two makers used this lack of knowledge as an opportunity for conversation and inclusiveness. During the half hour that I sat with these makers, eight different attendees approached them to hear an explanation of the work. None of these folks knew what a mezuzah was, and the project explanation became a conversation about the relationship between mezuzah as a cultural artifact and the technical design process involved in building an electronic, computational object. One of the makers explained:

> So, there's a Jewish tradition, there's a verse that says, "take these words and put them on the doorpost of your house."
>
> So, that's the commandment that was written into the Torah, so it's been around for 3,000 years. Over the years, people have been interacting with the tradition, as they walk through their homes and

have these [mezuzahs] on their doorposts, they would touch it, and they would give their hand a kiss.

We've taken that tradition one step further, and we have this device that detects someone at the door and starts reminding you what to do. So, when you touch it, it senses the touch.

These conversations served as opportunities for a meaning-making process at the intersection of cultural and technical knowing and doing that combined STEM education-like topics and intense personal interests. In order to understand why the mezuzah works the way it does, technically, people have to understand its cultural meaning and importance. And, in order to see how culture is represented in an object, it is important to see how the thing is made. In this case, discussions about what a mezuzah is connected seamlessly to a technical conversation about how the tiny computer (makers tend to use Arduino boards) connects the sensor on the door to the capacitor that stores electricity, so that your hand can communicate with the Mezuzah. The makers combined the Mezuzah and traditional songs as cultural artifacts and comedy tropes about anthropomorphized objects (the Mezuzah! It talks!) with the engineering and technology knowledge needed to build their working prototype. They engaged in a cycle of conceiving, representing, and sharing, and they were able to get feedback from a legitimate audience of other makers who were fascinated by the cultural features and familiar with the technical specifications.

There has been an explosion of interest in making and the Maker Movement as creating possibilities for connecting STEM education to a broader audience, including students left behind by the existing STEM pipeline. But Maker educators face the same challenge that STEAM proponents do—the urge to instrumentalize making in service of accountability measures, such as science content recall or workforce development, without attention to the epistemic practices that STEM and the arts share. This is especially problematic for students who have, historically, been left out; maker researchers and educators aim to use making to challenge and not reproduce inequities (Bevan et al., 2019).

A clear solution is to embrace the asset-based approach of culturally sustaining pedagogies into STEM education (Ryoo & Calabrese Barton, 2018). Paulo Blikstein calls this approach "cultural making," which he describes as a balance between respecting the local culture and context and the introduction of new elements that teachers or designers bring to the learning setting. This balance is itself contextual. In the United States, learning how to make our own stuff is often seen as an act of liberation, a way to get behind the curtain of industrialization. By contrast, Blikstein tells the story of Fatma, a Bedouin woman for whom buying food at the grocery store was empowering, a way to free her from the time-consuming practice of making her own cheese.

Cultural making should not be about romanticization of the *local* or simplistic incorporation of cultural elements into the production of objects. Cultural making should not be about uncritically importing academic agendas that do not fully understand learning and education or ignoring that youth culture around the world does not always follow the calcified, same-old views of US-centric "revolutionary" researchers. It should be about powerfully engaging youth with the political, human, and social challenges of subverting and transforming one's reality through powerful tools and representations. (2020, p. 125)

Cultural making is on display at the Embodied Physics Learning Lab, a community arts outreach program working with young, African American dancers (Solomon et al., in press). In this program, choreography is a mechanism to both understand and represent the principles of physics through the medium of modern dance. In creating the dance pieces, choreographer-performers have to (1) identify the principles of science they want to understand and express, such as the differences among elements in the periodic table, (2) use the tools of various dance forms—ballet, modern, krumping—to re-inscribe the features of different elements, and (3) rely on their cultural, embodied knowledge of how dance "works" to express their ways in which elements interact with one another. Peppler, Keune, and Thompson (2020) have written about how the fiber arts (weaving, crafting, crocheting) can be used to teach mathematics and computing. Since the fiber arts require working with your hands to construct representations of mathematical concepts, young people explore and engage in meaning-making across both arts and STEM practices, all while valuing the cultural contributions of traditionally feminine art forms. Cultural making allows young people to develop and express innovative ways of knowing, doing, and being. Communities like the Embodied Physics Learning Lab and electronic fiber arts programs redefine disciplinary boundaries by seeing the physics in dance and the math in weaving. What's more, these examples do not ask communities that have been marginalized in schools to define themselves in terms of STEM but, rather, demand that STEM acknowledge what they bring to the table.

ACT III: PUTTING THE ARTS AT THE CENTER

Most of the examples of successful STEAM and Maker programs that I've talked about have resisted instrumentalization, first in the face of the accountability machine and then within STEM. We can look to these informal learning environments for how to engage in the kind of programs that center the arts in learning (Mejias et al., 2021). These programs are often labeled as "out-of-school-time" (OST), even though arts programs often cross boundaries into school spaces both after school and during school hours. And they are worth talking about for how they might provide models to transform in-school learning, because the folks who run them play a huge role in establishing the value of arts learning for kids and communities. Also, this is where I have done the majority of my research and my own arts practice. So, it feels a little like I'm inviting you into my home. Grab a comfy chair.

OST arts programs are a mixed bag of nonprofit and community arts organizations, youth-serving organizations with arts programming, museums, government agencies, self-organized communities, and school-based programming with informal educators. All of these programs have strong opinions about the role of arts in learning and life. Most of these opinions have nothing to do with test scores, the achievement gap, or school subjects. There is freedom to the OST label that allows arts organizations to establish their own norms and values. While they often have to provide program evaluations to keep stakeholders happy, they are not beholden to the many requirements that accompany public schooling, including demonstrating that everything they do feeds reading and math or STEM goals. As you might imagine, this freedom is often useful to young people who may struggle in school but who flourish in OST arts settings. They can try on the alternative selves of artists and producers in OST spaces rather than as failures and troublemakers. An OST can be a whoopensocker of a learning environment!

Manchester Craftsmen's Guild (MCG) in Pittsburgh has been educating and inspiring youth through the arts since 1968. Founder Bill Strickland started out with a small ceramics studio for urban youth who could not afford arts education. Now, the program offers arts training in four disciplines—ceramics, design arts, digital arts, and photography—and the youth programs share space with a professional jazz music venue and an adult career-training institution. MCG is one of the few arts programs to "scale up"; there are National Centers for Art and Technology all over the world that take this approach. MCG describes the relationship between school and OST as "symbiotic." Rather than trying to make school look more like OST arts or OST arts look more like school, they let each fly its own flag. They do not reject school and academic outcomes, but rather relegate them to the school context:

> We firmly believe that the typical ways that schools track student achievement are not well-suited to measure success in afterschool learning environments . . . these numbers lack the ability to describe the powerful transformations of students as individuals and contributing members of MCG's learning community. (Green & Kindseth, 2011, p. 338)

We can learn a lot about how to center the arts in schools by looking at the ways in which OST arts-based learning environments have managed their design processes for teaching and learning. In large part, this is because OST arts programs did not interact with the accountability machine from Act I. What if young people who struggle with mainstream academics could be allowed to flourish by engaging in artistic production tasks? My friend Jack, who loved performing stories in class more than seeing his story "The Joe" performed in front of his whole school by professional actors, would be so much better served if his contributions to Whoopensocker City were valued in the same way as his math scores. In fact, one of the main reasons the "a" in STEAM offers so much promise is precisely because young people can meaningfully bring their strengths into academic tasks. The Maker Movement is, in large part, about valuing the arts as a way to leverage peoples' strengths, interests, and insights to solve problems and build community (Ryoo & Calabrese Barton, 2018).

Perhaps more importantly, arts practices are a vehicle for social justice. Some would argue simply bringing the arts to all kids is itself an act of social justice, of subverting a dominant narrative that the only kids who deserve the arts are those who have earned them or can afford them. And without the arts "children and youth experience an educational injustice whereby their future abilities to participate equally in the economic, cultural, and civic life of society are undermined" (Kraehe et al., 2016, p. 222). Beyond that, we also know that when the arts are brought into our teaching and learning practices, we are actively encouraging young people to fight for what they care about, to make change in the world, and to celebrate their own excellence and beauty. And while the arts are not a necessary condition for a social-justice movement, celebrating your own excellence and beauty in a system that tells you that you are less-than can be challenging. And exhausting. The arts bring joy to this difficult task.

CHAPTER 7

Taking the Arts to School

In my life as an arts educator and as the mayor of Whoopensocker City, I have brought the arts to schools for the past 25 years. And while these efforts have been meaningful, they have been modest. Here I have loftier aspirations: I want to give all of you the tools to center the arts in your learning environments. It is crucial that these takeaways be art-centric, and not generic best practices for the classroom. And I certainly don't want you to bring the arts into your classroom simply in service of raising test scores or making science experiments look prettier. I don't want you to put a bird on it. I want us to save education together through using arts-based learning and teaching practices across all of our learning environments. I am sharing a version of an arts integration strategy that will allow educators around the world to begin to use arts-based practices in their learning spaces. I offer three synthesizing big ideas that are arts-centric and can be taken up across learning environments as a way to reinvigorate our work with learners, especially those who have been left behind by inflexible institutional structures. Each idea has components of the learning outcomes, teaching strategies, and design principles that took up most of this book's real estate.

BIG IDEA 1: HONOR RISK-TAKING AS A CORE FEATURE OF TEACHING AND LEARNING

This seems like a good time to remind you of the Halverson adage:

The key to good teaching is scaffolding risk-taking.

Now that we've made it to the end, I want to take this idea further. Reframing teaching as arts practice puts risk-taking at the center of all teaching and learning. Notice that this doesn't require you as a teacher to see yourself as an artist or to be an artist but, rather, to acknowledge that teaching and learning is a cycle of improvisation and risk-taking. I say that because I know that folks are very hesitant to call themselves artists, and even more hesitant to bring their skills and values as artmakers into a classroom. So, let me show you how improv can restructure a learning experience in order to scaffold risk-taking and set up a productive learning environment.

Putting In and Taking Away

I start all of my classes—whether they be traditional college classes, professional development experiences with peers, or workshops with young artists—with a ritual. I know, I know. You *hate* icebreakers. Everyone does. But that's because doing an icebreaker just because you think you should doesn't work. An icebreaker that doesn't actively invite people in doesn't work either. Neither does something you do once and then never return to. You have to create rituals that invite learners to participate until it becomes a regular part of your classroom community. I almost always start by inviting everyone to share something that is distracting them from being fully present during our time together. I explain that this is to (1) acknowledge that we all have stuff that we bring to a learning space, (2) get whatever it is out of our heads and into the world, (3) try to put it aside for the duration of our time together, and (4) find out a little about the people who you are sharing space with. I also explain that what you share need not be a deep, dark secret. Most people say things like, "I'm distracted by the fact that my parents are coming to visit for the weekend after this class is over," or, "I'm distracted by the paper that is due for another class by the end of the day, and I haven't started it." There will also be some overlaps among people—"I'm also distracted by that paper I haven't started." But there will also be some unique information shared: "I'm getting a puppy next week, and I can't stop thinking about it." What people share will also get more personal over time, like, "My kid is sick, and I'm thinking about how they're doing at home," or, "My partner got a new job, and we have to move, and there's so much to do!" Another interesting phenomenon across time is that more and more people will come into the space, and say, "I'm not distracted by anything today—I'm excited to start working!" While this should not be an expectation (life is complicated, and everyone has commitments outside of our learning environments), I have seen over and over how knowing that you have an opportunity to share what's distracting you begins to prepare you to not be distracted.

There is a second part to this ritual. At the end of every session, each person has to take something with them from our time together that they will carry forward. Again, no need for super-deep takeaways. People often take something that made them laugh or feel good. Usually, that's something that someone else did or said, which creates a connection between them and has the side effect of making the person who said or did the funny thing feel good. As time goes on, the takeaways tend to get more serious; they focus on the hard ideas from the class, rather than on surface features of peoples' actions: "I am taking Jonathan's model of Black, male identity that he presented," or "I'm taking an understanding of 'epistemology' as a way of describing what counts as knowledge." For those of you who are in teacher-school, you can see these takeaways as public "exit slips"—a popular way of informally gauging student understanding at the end of class.

Every Learning Experience Begins with What Learners Bring to the Space. Why is this ritual of putting in and taking away so powerful? This is a practical and very simple method of engaging in asset-based pedagogy. It is the opposite of a pre-test, designed to measure where people fall short of the goals we have for them. Instead, it is the foundation for valuing each learner as a necessary and productive member of your learning environment. Bringing excitement about your new puppy to our time together? Great—let's figure out how the new puppy can be a part of our math lesson. Anxiety about that unfinished English paper? Let this class time be an opportunity to open up your thinking. And if you need your peers to step up this session, because your brain is on Fortnite and algebra, you can let them know. This is also an opportunity to remind people that every day is not a "best day ever" for every person. We put so much pressure on ourselves to be our best all the time; bringing yourself into a learning space allows us, collectively, to figure out who is having one of their best days ever and can be relied upon to carry the weight of the class. It is also a way to learn who has what expertise that can be leveraged in the context of a particular learning environment. When someone says they are distracted by "that video I was editing for my YouTube channel where I play through new Sims game packs," you think, "Aha! This person knows a whole bunch of things that I don't. I can ask them for video-editing advice, or just find out more about what the Sims game is like in 2021." Learners (especially kids) are constantly told what they are lacking as a starting point for any new learning experience. It's demoralizing and not a super inspiring way to start something new. "Putting in" starts with what people bring and takes it from there.

There Are No Right Answers, and It Is Okay to Cheat! Since we are asking everyone to bring their distractions, it is rarely (if ever) hard to think of something to say. People who *are* nervous and don't want to say the wrong thing are free to use what the person before them has said. "They stole mine!" is a common and unifying refrain among folks when they take something away at the end of class time. Sometimes, what happens is collaborative—people pick up others' ideas, "Yes, and," them, and create a new takeaway that extends the original. This is the gradual release model (I do; we do; you do), as an act of collaboration in action. A "collaboration through the air," if you will. I start by sharing something of myself. (Usually, I put in my nervous-citement about starting a new learning environment on the first day. Admitting that I'm nervous-cited is part of scaffolding risk.) Then each person's contribution becomes part of the "we do," and those who feel more able can shoulder a larger part of the load. Someone who is uncomfortable speaking English in a public setting, for example, can use what another person said, or just say, "I agree with her." Since the whole process happens out loud, everyone gets to hear this collaborative chain; while each individual puts in or takes away something different, the collective gets to take all of it in one way or another. Everyone participates. All contributions are equally valued.

Scaffolding Risk-Taking Takes Time and Commitment That You May Not Think You Have. In education, we have been trained to focus on content, to make sure we "cover" everything, and to minimize peoples' "off-task" behavior. But learners can smell when you don't actually care what they are bringing into the learning environment or what you are taking away. Putting in and taking away is not fluff; it's essential to a successful learning experience. At Whoopensocker, we warm up for 15–20 minutes at the start of every rehearsal, regardless of how much we have to get done or how short we are on time, because knowing who we are and what we bring to the rehearsal room is essential, both to making good art and to our collective humanity. Listening to everyone's contributions takes time, and it is time worth spending. It is not extra, or the lead-up to learning, it *is* the learning. Which means each time you come together, folks need the opportunity to talk about how they are coming in—no skimping. While it is particularly essential in the beginning of your time with a group, consistency and rules are (as you know) part of any good arts-based learning environment. Do it. Stick with it. Make it core to what it means to teach and learn.

Variations on a Theme

This ritual has tons of variations, some of which are worth mentioning here. You don't have to feel constrained by the "putting in and taking away" concept—that may be too mature for your learners, or just plain boring. You should use the kind of practice that is both authentic to you and to the group of learners that you are working with. So, here are some ways that I build on this general idea (and how you can too!):

> *Bring an Object to Share.* People like to use their sense of touch, a sense we typically limit in many learning settings. The arts are inherently haptic[1] in nature, so I always try to bring touch into my learning designs. I like to bring an object that is special to me and pass it around as a turn-taking mechanism. I have a piece of ceramic art shaped like a small pillow decorated with a hen that I absolutely love (yeah, I know, I put a bird on it). I often bring it with me to a space as an object to pass around. I make it known that it is special to me, because it can "hold" a lot of distractions at once. Touching

an object makes people feel connected, and the person with the object commands the space.

Let's Get Physical. When I work with groups that I know are either more ready to take a risk or are likely to be in situations where they will have to take risks (looking at you, future teachers), I sometimes move from the haptic to the physical. For example, a group can build a fire—not literally, that's a safety hazard— through mimed actions and sound effects. With 30 people, you can get quite a roaring fire going. Then you throw what's distracting you into the fire, and it lights up in a puff of imagined smoke with a verbalized explosion. When you're done, you can reduce the fire to pocket-sized (another advantage of mimed fire), and put it in the corner of the room, or in someone's pocket to simmer throughout class. You can bring it out at the end and allow peoples' takeaways to rise like phoenices[2] from the ashes. There are tons of other physicalized ways to put in and take away—if you can dream it, you can build it.

The Gift That Keeps on Giving. The two variations above don't require any individualized interaction among people. Groups build up to wanting or needing to have people speak directly to each other. It's amazing how infrequently we offer this opportunity in learning spaces. A low-key way to have interpersonal interaction that also values Indigenous communities' arts practices is through gift giving (Barajás-Lopez & Bang, 2018). I learned this variation recently from my student/colleague/friend Kailea, when we tried to figure out how to start a working group via videoconference. The person who initiates the game says something along the lines of, "Kailea, I am so happy that you are here, today, and I would like to give you this gift." Kailea takes the gift (it can be physical, mimed, or not at all), and says, "Thanks, Erica. I really need . . ."—insert something she needs in order to get through her time in the learning environment that day—"this pass for someone to sit next to me during our small-group time who understood the readings, because I'm struggling." Onto the next: "Andy, I haven't seen you all week, so I thought I'd bring you a gift." "Thanks, Kai! I really need this pair of socks, because my feet are freezing!" While gift giving allows individuals to interact, everyone is still in charge of what and how much they share. The giver gives neutrally and waits for the receiver to say what they need.

Three Things! (and Other, More Complicated Sharing) I use my favorite game—Three Things!—as a framework for the three main design principles for arts-based learning environments. Before it was a framework, it was a warm-up game that I frequently play with groups to get them ready to work. You can use this version, too, as a way to scaffold risk-taking. It can be as straightforward as everyone putting in three things that are distracting them—recall that each "thing" still gets feedback from the whole group in the form of "One! Two! Three things!" Or, you can get fancy and allow the giver to improvise what three things they want someone to put in. It can be totally open-ended, or you can keep it constrained to the school space: "Three assignments you wish you didn't have!" Or, "Your three favorite classes ever!" Or, "Three things you learned this semester!" My point is, a game like this can achieve the same aims as putting in and taking away, while affording learners additional agency.

Get Loud. For those of you who work with our youngest learners, you may think that all of this language play and focus on learning needs is out of reach. I get it. While I have known many 4-year-olds who can tell you exactly what they need in order to be successful, this may not be the most exciting way to start a learning task with a group of young learners. To that I say: Whoopensocker warm-up games to the rescue. You can achieve this same goal with a simple "sound and movement game." There are a gazillion variations on this game, but the basic way is to have kids make a sound and do a movement. A jump with a "Yahoo!", a fist pump accompanied by "Yes!", or a fall onto the ground with a grunt, are all sound-and-movement combinations that show up regularly. A "dabbing" motion accompanied by the word "dab" was super popular among the Whoopensocker set for about 3 years. This can be done as call and response (someone does a sound and movement, and everyone does it back), as a round robin (someone does a sound and movement, and then it ripples around the whole group until it comes back to the originator), with names (you say your name with a movement), posing a question (give me a sound and movement that describes how you feel right now), and so on. This beginning ritual allows kids to (1) participate early, (2) know it's okay to try something different out, (3) do the same thing a person before them did, if they are too nervous to come up with something independently, and (4) prepare to try out more challenging tasks. The first few times might be bumpy, but once it's part of the routine, kids will come to expect this as the way they come into a learning space.

This should always be part of every learning environment. Scaffolding risk-taking right at the beginning of the learning activity through play is the best pedagogical strategy to set the tone for constructivist learning.

BIG IDEA 2: EMBRACE EMBRACE IDENTITY AND REPRESENTATION AS-CORE IDEAS, BUT DO NOT MISTAKE ONE FOR THE OTHER

The arts allow people to explore, discover, embrace and critique representations as the core activity of learning. When learners are making representations, they are making their learning process visible for teachers and for one another. Moving beyond representations as conversational turns (e.g., answers to questions) to external artifacts invites learners to create more comprehensive accounts of what they know. Asking learners to show what they mean in a dance or a picture creates many points of entry for feedback and critique, and provides a stable foundation for creating new representations that reflect feedback and refine understanding. Revisiting homework is a good way to build meaningful representations into the day-to-day work of the classroom, provided the feedback given is prompt and can lead to a new version of the artifact. Sequencing representations as progressive understandings of key ideas allows for the use of representational trajectories as tools for assessment. Building a regular schedule of multimodal representations into classwork, and designing the representations so that the work is meaningful to other students and, when possible, to a wider audience outside the class, opens up classrooms to this primary artmaking practice as a powerful everyday tool for learning.

Representation is the single most important concept that arts learning can bring to educational change. Teachers can invite students to participate in the representational trajectory around the content of their choice; we have seen throughout this book how representation is a core part of learning in science, math, language arts, and social studies. The ideas being represented can be conceptual, like creating flow or understanding chemical reactions. They can also be practical, like creating models for a new playground. If you take one thing from our time together, it's that the arts show us how crucial representations are to learning.

While representation stretches across all schooling disciplines, arts learning typically features identity as a focus of representation. In arts programs, we typically begin by asking people to represent themselves, their lives, or issues and questions that matter to them. We do that because the arts lend themselves naturally to questions about self, and there are otherwise very few opportunities to explore ideas about yourself in an organized learning setting. Advocates for culturally responsive pedagogy describe how kids who had been marginalized from school often choose the arts as their outlet for self-expression. For many young people, making art is a life-sustaining practice (Wong & Peña, 2017). As a result, it is important to recognize how crucial representations of identity are to redesigning education for all learners, and especially for those for whom school has been a hostile place. Using the representational trajectory around identity is a powerful mechanism for engaging in a culturally sustaining, asset-based approach to teaching and learning.

Not All "Identity Work" Is Positive

Using artmaking to manage the institutional and historical challenges of schooling means that not all representations are based on rosy stories of triumphing over adversity. Identity development can allow students to differentiate from mainstream culture: Writing stories that express negative opinions about political leaders, designing and printing a weapon in an open-ended making session, and writing and performing a play that highlights the tension between alternative gender identities and family traditions are all productive and transgressive expressions of identity.

We see this often in Whoopensocker. Because we tell kids that "every idea is a good idea," and we mean it, we open up space for them to talk about the transgressive parts of themselves that they are usually asked to check at the school door. Over the years, I have read thousands and thousands of stories by 8- and 9-year-olds. A lot of them are true stories, where kids reflect on the violence they see in their communities—school shootings, parents in prison, cousins who lost their lives in gang-related activity. We only rarely include these stories in performance because it feels like we would be breaking the trust we've earned with the writers. We do, occasionally, hear these stories read out loud by kids in classrooms, but most of the time we dialogue with the writers on paper. We acknowledge that we've read what they have to say, tell them that their experiences are valid, and thank them for sharing with us. Kids also write about fictionalized violence constantly, both as a way to "try on" ideas about engaging with others in a physically violent way, and because they are so often told this is not something that is appropriate for school. We sometimes perform these stories, especially if they feature characters like unicorns fighting The Rock or John Cena (an enduringly popular way to enact comedic violence). Kids are also obsessed with potty-related stories. I told you that all of us in Whoopensocker love poop jokes. This true story will not disappoint. It is one of my all-time faves:

> When my little sister was 3 and I was 5, my brother was eating chocolate chips. My little sister asked him what he was eating, so he spit it out and said, "I'm eating poops." So, my little sister asked my mom, "Can I have some poops?" But my mom said, "No." So, she stood up on the chair and starting yelling, "I want some poops," and mom said, "We don't serve poops at this house." "But Brian has some," my sister said. "Okay," my mom said. "I want some poops," she said. "Poops go in the potty. Why don't you play with Alison? Alison, what are you doing?" [my mom said]. "Something," I said.[3]

We often perform these kinds of stories, partly because we find them hilarious (have I already mentioned how much I love a good poop joke?)

and partly because we want to honor the transgressive nature of kid humor. When we do, the stories become disconnected from the person's identity in a way that honors the idea but does not tie the individual directly to the representation.

Try "Representing the Other"

So, how do you engage your learners in identity-related performance work without having to be a professional theater artist, hip-hop artist, or film-maker? I want to share another baseline activity—what I call "represent-ing the other"—as a mechanism for remaking learning environments for everyone. When I was in graduate school, I talked my advisors into letting me take a research-methods class in the performance studies department, because I knew that I wanted to think about the role of the arts in research, even as I was becoming a social scientist. The instructor, Dwight Conquer-good, was an ethnographer (and a remarkable human being) who used live performance as the primary mechanism for communicating his research findings. For context, probably the most famous performance ethnographer is Anna Deavere Smith, whose one-woman shows *Fires in the Mirror*, *Twi-light: Los Angeles*, and the more recent *Notes from the Field* are some of the finest examples of the intersection of art and primary source research. Just like with putting in and taking away, I use a version of an activity I learned in Dwight's class in almost every learning environment that I lead.

The assignment is simple. Everyone gets a partner, preferably someone they do not know. They begin by spending a minimum of 1 hour just getting to know one another. Many people will balk at this—they'll feel anxious about spending 60 minutes with a stranger. But once they get into the idea of just being together, it goes by quickly. And more often than not, people end up spending even more time with each other. After that, each person has to create a representation of the other person, using whatever media or tools they choose, and then share that representation with the class.

Of course, many people will panic when you tell them they have to cre-ate something. So, I often give a range of examples of the kinds of things I have seen people produce over the years—songs, meals, collages, Facebook profiles, clothing, PowerPoint presentations—I once had a student (who happened to be a priest) engage the class in a longform improvisation by recreating the bar where he met his partner. We drank and talked together like old friends and learned about the pair who had gotten to know one another earlier that week. I tell people that it is important to choose repre-sentations that you think fit the person you are getting to know and to think about the superpowers you possess that could help you complete the assign-ment. I also tell people that they can work together on their representation, if that feels the most authentic to their conversation. (I'd say pairs team up about 10% of the time.) This is best done as a homework assignment where people first have the time to spend with one another, and then have more time for reflection and creation. And here's the best part: No one ever blows it. Unless the person decides to drop the class (which happens sometimes in higher education, and they almost always tell me they are sad about not getting to complete this assignment), everyone brings in something. For some people, this represents a slow walk to the freedom of drawing on a broader range of representational resources than they have typically been given in school. For others, they create as if they've just been waiting for someone to ask them to make an interactive map that shows the many places their partner has lived and what is important to them about those places.

Sharing these representations back with the class is a nonnegotiable part of the assignment. And, while sharing functions as an assessment and an opportunity for critique, it primarily serves as a way for people to see what and how others share about them in a public space. What information do people choose to include? What kinds of representations do they come up with? What kinds of joys do the group take from learning about new friends from someone else? And it sure beats having to introduce yourself. About that, I think we can all agree.

The Audience Learns as Much About the Person Doing the Representing as They Do About the Person Being Represented. I have led this activity at least 100 times since I took Dwight's class back before the turn of the century. So, I have something to say about the big takeaways that people have from participating in this activity. First, the choice of medium often tells the audience a lot. Someone who writes songs will often be inclined to write a song about their partner. While the song is a great package for telling the audience about someone, it is also a sign of the kind of artist (and human) that the writer is. But the best part is that if that person was asked to talk about themselves, they likely wouldn't mention it, and we certainly wouldn't learn about their songwriting superpower. Who brings their guitar to class or records a song on GarageBand to introduce themselves? It only works if you're writing about someone else.

A few years ago, I ran this activity during an early career symposium for academics—really smart adults with tons of informed opinions about how to structure effective learning environments. After it was over, my friend, math education professor José Gutiérrez, wrote to me about the activity and reflected on how much the representation centered him, rather than his partner:

> I realized that every element I chose to include in the representation was something personally, deeply meaningful to me. From the "thinking man" to "Me vs. You" to the "2038 Dope Life Awards," these were all things that *I* could relate to and had thought about previously or had ever written about. . . . During the interview, G and

Sketch by José Gutiérrez as he prepared his "Representing the Other."

Reprinted with permission of the artist.

I discussed a number of things, yet *I* made the decision as to what to represent about him, how to interpret those representations, and how to perform them for an audience. Thus, the representation was less about G and more (all?) about me.

Representing someone else is as much an activity of representing ourselves, minus the fear and anxiety that comes with having to choose what to share of yourself. But there's also the weight of the power that comes with choosing what to share about someone else and some anxiety that, in choosing what to share, you may reveal your own self-centeredness.

Representations Almost Always Focus on the Intersections Between Partners. This is true of the content as well as the form. If one person loves rock climbing, it is not unusual for the other person's fear of heights to come out in conversation and to see that fear represented in the final product. This happens even if the person who is afraid of heights would not typically share that trait when describing themselves. Or if both people have moved a lot in their lives, I would not be surprised to see two very similar representations (typically, maps with some sort of "life is a journey" metaphor built in). As a result, a bond typically forms between partners that endures throughout the life of the learning experience and the pair often pursues a collective line of inquiry that they otherwise might not have.

One student in my *This American Life* class perfectly captured the class's collective response: "Kayla represented me, and her description of me was absolutely phenomenal. She pointed out things about myself that I didn't even know but were true. She captured the true essence of who I am and how I wish to be portrayed." When you ask people how it feels to be represented, they almost always say something like this. Seeing yourself through someone else's eyes opens up new possibilities for how you see yourself, how others see you, and your potential for fitting into a learning community.

Finally, representing someone else validates your own creative choices as part of what it means to learn. It is very common for students, especially anyone over about age 11, to tell you that they are "not creative," or "not good at art." But the freedom to represent someone however you choose, and the chance to be critiqued rather than criticized, frequently shows people that they should lean into their creative impulses, rather than lament the impulses they lack. I once had a student who insisted that she could not do anything arts-related. This caused her great anxiety, because she was planning to become an early childhood educator, and she had to take my arts integration class to get there. Through her partner work, she revealed that she loved to knit tiny monsters—finger-puppet-sized, cartoon-like objects. Her partner convinced her to use that skill as the method of representation (I think that was partly selfish, because the partner *really* wanted some of those monsters for herself). This skill became a cornerstone of the person's arts integration work, and (hopefully) guides her teaching practice now, 8 years later.

I recognize that the phrase "the other" might be problematic, here. I don't disagree—"othering" people has a bad history in our public school systems, and our public discourse more generally. However, the idea of "other" allows us to start with the concept that we are representing something that isn't us—another person, the idea of flow, the phenomenon of AIDS as a public health crisis, or the equations needed to build the monkey bars—even as we end up with something about ourselves and our shared experiences. In reflecting on his use of this activity in his own classes, José told me:

> Usually, someone observes that about half the interviewees brought up race and racial identity and made it into the representations. However, typically about half of the pairs do not mention anything about race, gender, sexual orientation, etc., as salient or relevant in their lives. The result is politically neutral representations. We then try to look at this

from different angles: how do my positionality and stance filter how I see my partner? What parts of my intersectional identity am I choosing to talk about, and why?

The use of the word "other" makes these questions relevant and exciting and gives us an open opportunity to talk about the othering we do all the time. I look forward to your answers.

Variations on a Theme

Just like with the putting-in and taking-away game, there are productive variations here that could better match your learning environments. I have done "representing the other" in a shorter time frame, even within one session. If you only have limited time, it helps to constrain the kinds of representational resources people can use. People typically have computers or phones with them, so you can encourage everyone to make something with their technology. Or, you can have supplies available, and make part of the challenge to represent the other person using only those materials. I have a suitcase of stuff that lives in my office that I have used for this purpose many times.

If you are concerned that this activity is too far from your content area (this is a history class, for Pete's sake!), you can make either the content or the process topical. You can, for example, assign people to learn about each other's family genealogies, and represent that. Or you can choose tools you imagine using in your course—maps for geography, poetry for language arts, symbols for math—and require that partners use only those to represent each other. No matter how you adapt this activity, embracing the power of representation and identity by making work about one another is a crucial way of reimagining learning through design.

BIG IDEA 3: TAKING COLLECTIVE RESPONSIBILITY

The last big idea I want to leave you with is a sense of collective, collaborative responsibility for learning. And I mean this in the true sense, not just in the group-project sense. We know that the learning outcomes of arts practice are all connected. Collaboration as an outcome results from a focus on identity (individual and collective), which is often the topic of our representational trajectories that typically involve a range of language practices. Nick's participation in Whoopensocker as a writer, a performer, and a costume designer is a great example of both individual learning outcomes and how these outcomes work together. It also highlights how the arts allow us to understand and value the learning ecology that Nick was a part of. This ecology includes his classroom teachers, Whoopensocker teaching artists, school rules and tools, arts practices, families and the other kids in the environment. Learning from the arts means embracing the ecology over the individual.

What Is a Learning Ecology?

The concept of a learning ecology describes the people, programs, places, practices, roles, tools, and goals that make up a person's learning world (Akiva et al., 2019; Barron, 2006). We all exist in learning ecologies, though schools typically do a poor job of acknowledging the ecologies of most students, unless they embrace an asset-pedagogies approach. And, despite the fact that the vast majority of our time is spent in informal learning settings, school takes up the vast majority of our collective energy. The LIFE Center[4] estimates that even at peak schooling time (K–12), school only accounts for about 18.5% of our learning time (Banks et al., 2007). But school is where all young people are, so when we think about doing teaching and learning differently to improve peoples' lives, those changes have to become a part of the school day. When it comes to an arts-based approach, a lack of arts-focused programming in schools has meant that the arts are often "choice-in," meaning kids have to sign up, show up, possibly pay for, or simply choose on their own to participate in arts practices. This only serves to widen the participation gap between those who are able to take part and those for whom structural barriers stand in their way (Kraehe et al., 2016).

You might be thinking there is some wisdom to keeping school separate from outside interests, especially for kids who have historically struggled; those who are seen as "bad students" may see connections between the arts practices they love and their school as crossing unwanted boundaries. Organizations like the Manchester Craftsmen's Guild have solved this problem, by developing a philosophy of peaceful coexistence: Schools do their thing, arts organizations do theirs (Green & Kindseth, 2011). There is real concern from kids, artists, and heck, from me, that arts practices will become colonized once they enter the school space; if we bring them into school, the accountability machine might devour us all.

But at this point in our journey together, I think we can agree that an arts-focused approach to schooling allows us the opportunity to move from choice-in to all-in: We recognize that it is people, programs, and tools working together that make teaching, learning, and design better. My own work on distributed instruction in youth media-arts organizations provides a theoretical justification for the power of learning ecologies (Halverson et al., 2015). There are some great examples of how this looks at a citywide scale. The Creative Learning initiative in Pittsburgh (Akiva et al., 2019), The Hive Network in New York City (Ching et al., 2015), and the Arts-Infusion Initiative in Chicago (Yahner et al., 2015) all demonstrate how a learning-ecologies approach can positively benefit kids' lives by giving them real opportunities for decision-making and accommodating varying comfort levels with collaborative artmaking. The best example of a successful learning ecology is the Digital Youth Network (DYN). DYN consists of a series of school-based curricula, public library–based after-school sites, and a digital platform for accessing projects and people from wherever kids are. And the best part about DYN? The arts are at the center of it all. None of the work would be possible without teaching artists, or a focus on the arts-based outcomes I have defined (Barron et al., 2014).

Who and What Is Part of the Learning Ecology?

Among the many terrific insights of the DYN project is the importance of including teaching artists in the learning ecology. The concept of a teaching artist—a professional artist who mentors others to develop their art form in an educational setting—has been around in American schools since the early 1970s. You will often see teaching artists hired into classrooms when a school, or a district, promotes arts integration as a model (Burnaford et al., 2007). Teaching artists can serve as either co-planners and instructors with classroom teachers, or engage as artists-in-residence, where they are taking the lead in working with students, while the classroom teacher serves more as a resource (Hardiman & John Bull, 2019). Teaching artists are also the backbone of youth arts organizations; many of the program examples I have shared throughout this book, including my own work with Whoopensocker, depend on teaching artists to co-create dynamic and meaningful arts learning experiences for young people. Teaching artists provide one solution to the "egg crate culture" of schools that keeps teachers and classroom practices isolated from one another (Graue et al., 2007).

Working in a collaborative learning ecology benefits everyone—classroom teachers, teaching artists, and students. Classroom teachers are relieved of the pressure of having to be expert in *everything*; a hip-hop artist can help you build a project that is grounded in hip-hop pedagogy. And this artist could come from anywhere in the community—a professional teaching artist hired by a service-provider agency, from a local university program, from the local community, or drawn straight from the families of your students. Many teaching artists are not experts in the pedagogical strategies and learning outcomes most classroom teachers have to focus on, so they benefit from ongoing partnerships with professionals. And both groups of adults learn from the young people who are typically put into the role of "learner," though we now know that young peoples' assets and expertise are core to setting expectations for what to produce and how to produce it. For young people, building relationships with professional artists is a formative part of creating identities in the community of artists in which they are collectively working.

Teaching artists, adults who do not have the classroom teacher designation, are typically paid less, have lower job security, and not often are accorded the label of "educator." Furthermore, many of these folks are young people of color (Akiva et al., 2019). Since our teaching workforce is overwhelmingly White, and our public school students are overwhelmingly not, figuring out a way to truly value the work of these teaching artists in facilitating arts practices as ways of teaching and learning is of the utmost importance.

How Do I Get a Learning Ecology?

So, say you are excited about arts-based learning. How do you get to be part of a learning ecology? At Whoopensocker, we have the benefit of being associated with a university as a mechanism for valuing the work of teaching artists in and out of the classroom. We are able to identify undergraduate and graduate students and community members who are practicing artists and train them through hands-on work with Whoopensocker and in more formal classroom experiences at the university. We then partner them with classroom teachers who are excited to bring these arts professionals into their classrooms. We are also able to fundraise for this program independently of school-based budgets, so that we take on some of the burden of paying for additional adults in the classroom. And our status as professional artists puts us in conversation with other artists in the community, so that we can take advantage of arts resources.

But you may not be a university professor—you are a teacher, a future teacher, or a parent. How do *you* help contribute to the creation of learning ecologies that support the arts-based ways of teaching and learning that we have been talking about?

Open Your Door. Literally and figuratively. Invite people into your classroom or your living room who have expertise in arts practices. Invite yourself into classrooms and afterschool programs to share your arts superpower. A nice initial step is to either partner with a teaching artist for the first time, or to figure out which community-arts organizations in your town offer programs where you could work. Figuratively, we can find connected learning ecologies for virtually every interest online. If you don't live in a place where you feel you have ready access to arts educators, connect to the Minecraft education community to see how teachers across the country have built academic challenges into online gaming. Or allow students to bring their own connected learning communities into the classroom. Currently, TikTok houses thousands of micro-communities with expertise in everything from beekeeping to World War I.

Value the Role of Artist-Educators. These are the folks "doing the work," and they deserve our respect. We need career paths that value the role of the teaching artist, and we need a cultural shift that acknowledges their irreplaceable value.

Leverage Kids' Expertise Across the Worlds They Occupy. A kid who
shines as a spoken-word poet could use those skills in their other
classes at school, likely even helping their classroom teachers use
spoken word successfully in the classroom. This is a positive way
to combine the various worlds that young people occupy. As a
corollary to opening your door, when you allow in kids' expertise,
together you can begin to build a learning ecology.

The arts show us that teaching, learning, and design are bigger than any
one teacher, curriculum, or test. Reimagining learning from the perspective
of an ecology allows us to embrace the distributed aspects of teaching and
learning to include everyone from public librarians to YouTubers, and to
value expertise for how it helps us to make work together.

EVERY IDEA IS A GOOD IDEA

We have come to the end of our journey, which takes us back to the beginning: The man who passed out who did not go to jail. Or the concert that
ended 15 minutes early. Through scaffolding risk-taking, creating representations that focus on each other's identities, and building learning ecologies
that include artists of all ages, we can imagine a future for education that is
inclusive, culturally sustaining, rigorous, and just plain joyful. While I am
not here to claim that Whoopensocker saved anyone's life, I witnessed first-
hand that kids like Nick, Jack, Lamar, Gustavo, and the writers of "Dear
Donald Trump," "Dear Michelle Obama," and even "Dear Future Vampire
Self" had their lives changed for the better. They brought their own expertise into the process, they worked alongside their peers to make something
collective, and their contributions were taken seriously by adults who earn
their living as artists. These are the gifts we can give as educators to make
school a place where kids want to spend their time, and see possibilities
for their own futures. It's also a roadmap for transforming education and
beginning a new era where we reject test scores as measures of success, and
embrace kids' assets rather than focus on their deficits. I don't know about
you, but this mayor is invigorated, full of joy, and ready for what comes
next. Fun is in the needs.

Notes

Chapter 1

1. This, like all names of kids and schools used throughout the book, is a pseudonym. But wouldn't it be great if this was actually the name of the school?

2. I love this word for all of its vowels. It means, "the works of a painter, composer, or author, regarded collectively," and I think it describes the collection quite well!

3. Throughout the book, I will share stories written by kids. These stories will either be presented as originally written or edited for grammar when the original phrasing impedes understanding. Where I have made changes, they are as minor as possible to keep the kids' writing intact.

4. If you prefer to call this "scatological humor" when you talk to your other grown-ups, feel free. I'm sticking with poop jokes.

Chapter 2

1. Benjamin Franklin would be so proud. He is credited with the quotable quote, "a place for everything and everything in its place." If you don't know, now you know.

2. Don Norman is a father of the human-centered design movement and has been writing about the role of artifacts as external representations since the late 1980s. He has said many brilliant things about external representations, and even has a chapter in his book on representations entitled "A place for everything and everything in its place." So we're basically twins.

3. The philosopher Alfred Korzybski is credited with a version of this statement, that "the map is not the territory."

4. In the rest of the book, I will use the word "representation" to refer to external representation, unless I want to highlight what is going on in a thinker's head.

5. Figuratively, not literally. We are literally on the same page.

6. Annie Lee was a painter known for her depictions of everyday life in African American communities. The book chapter we wrote has prints of the Annie Lee paintings that were used in this curricular intervention (Lee et al., 2004).

7. Also sometimes called African American Vernacular English and Black Vernacular English.

Chapter 3

1. Project Zero is the biggest research center on Art and Education in the United States. They have tons of great resources and projects, most of which you can access for free: www.pz.harvard.edu.

2. Sexton's Wikipedia entry references two documentaries featuring his banjo playing. There is also great information on the history of banjo playing in south central Kentucky from the Lomax Project, http://culturalequity.org.

Chapter 4

1. His best friend. This one is a joke.

2. Sorry to shout. I sometimes get worked up. No one will ever accuse me of lacking passion.

Chapter 5

1. I guess it's possible you just flipped right to this page in hopes that you would find something magical inside, especially if you are my dad. He once told me that I should put a $20 bill inside the printed copy of my dissertation, and then go back, and check it, periodically, to see if the bill was still there. If it was, no one had read my dissertation. Dad, here's your proverbial $20 bill. I look forward to your text telling me you've read this book.

2. This is part of a longer interview on storytelling, posted on YouTube over 10 years ago: https://www.youtube.com/watch?v=dx2cI-2FJRs. Ain't he smart?

3. I have literally looked there. You can visit the Loris Magaluzzi International Centre in Reggio Emilia that focuses exclusively on the Reggio approach to schooling (www.reggiochildren.it/en/loris-malaguzzi-international-centre/).

Chapter 6

1. Fun fact: The original acronym was SMET, which I think is funnier, and, therefore, I like it more. I can't find any documentation on why it was changed other than that it didn't sound good (Mejias et al., 2021). I think SMET sounds like something weird that you spread on toast whereas STEM involves metaphors of roots and plants. So, I guess I'll forgive the change.

2. There is a great interview with the co-creators of the sketch, Carrie Brownstein and Fred Armisen, where they talk about the origin of this idea: https://www.nytimes.com/video/multimedia/100000002897838/8216portlandia8217-put-a-bird-on-it.html

Chapter 7

1. The 50-cent word for any form of interaction involving touch. I love the way it looks and sounds. Also, it gives you one word where you sometimes need a whole phrase.

2. Yup, that's the plural of phoenix. I looked it up. Although, according to legend, only one phoenix lives at any given time, so there isn't really much call for the use of phonecies. Until now!

3. I have added punctuation to make it clearer who is speaking to whom!

4. The Learning in Informal and Formal Environments (LIFE) Center is a multi-institutional partnership housed at the University of Washington, dedicated to the study of life-long, life-wide, and life-deep learning (Banks et al., 2007).

References

Adjapong, E. S. & Emdin, C. (2015). Rethinking pedagogy in urban spaces: Implementing hip-hop pedagogy in the urban science classroom. *Journal of Urban Learning Teaching and Research,11*, 66–77.

Akiva, T., Hecht, M., & Osai, E. (2019). *Creative learning in Pittsburgh*. The Heinz Endowments.

Alvermann, D. (2017). Media literacies. In K. Peppler (Ed.), *The SAGE encyclopedia of out-of-school learning*, (pp . 472–475). SAGE Publications, Inc.

Anderson, T., & Shattuck, J. (2012). Design-based research: A decade of progress in education research? *Educational Researcher, 41*(1), 16–25.

Arts Education Partnership (U.S.), Deasy, R., Catterall, J. S., Hetland, L., & Winner, E. (2002). Critical links: Learning in the arts and student academic and social development. Arts Education Partnership.

Au, W. (2011). Teaching under the new Taylorism: High-stakes testing and the standardization of the 21st-century curriculum. *Journal of Curriculum Studies, 43*(1), 25–45.

Banks, J., Au, K., Ball, A. F., Bell, P., Gordon, E., Gutierrez, K., Brice-Heath, S., Lee, C. D., Mahiri, J., Nasir, N., Valdes, G., & Zhou, M. (2007). *Learning in and out of school in diverse environments: Life-long, life-wide, life-deep*. The LIFE Center (University of Washington, Stanford University, and SRI) & the Center for Multicultural Education, University of Washington.

Barajas-Lopez, F., & Bang, M. (2018). Indigenous making and sharing: Claywork in an Indigenous STEAM program. *Equity & Excellence in Education, 51*(1), 7–20.

Barker, L., & Borko, H. (2011). Conclusion: Presence and the art of improvisational teaching. In K. Sawyer (Ed.), *Structure and improvisation in creative teaching*, (pp. 278–298). Cambridge University Press.

Barron, B. (2006). Interest and self-sustained learning as catalysts of development: A learning ecology perspective. *Human Development, 49*(4), 193–224.

Barron, B., Gomez, K., Pinkard, N., & Martin, C. K. (2014). *The digital youth network: Cultivating digital media citizenship in urban communities*. MIT Press.

Bass, M. B. & Halverson, E. R. (2013). Representing self through media: A personal journey through *This American Life*. In K. Jocson (Ed.), *Cultural transformations: Youth and pedagogies of possibility* (pp. 79–96). Harvard Education Press.

Beghetto, R. A., & Kaufman, J. C. (2007). Toward a broader conception of creativity: A case for "mini-c" creativity. *Psychology of Aesthetics, Creativity in the Arts, 1*(2), 73–79.

Bevan, B. Peppler, K., Rosin, M., Scarff, L., Soep, L., & Wong, J. (2019). Purposeful pursuits: Leveraging the epistemic practices of the arts and sciences. In A. J. Stewart, M. P. Mueller, and D. J. Tippins (Eds.), *Converting STEM into STEAM programs: Methods and examples from and for education* (pp. 21–38). Springer.

Blikstein, P. (2020). Cheesemaking emancipation: The critical theory of cultural making. In N. Holbert, M. Berland, & Y. Kafai (Eds.), *Designing constructionist futures: The art, theory, and practice of learning designs* (pp. 115–126). MIT Press.

Bowen, D. H., & Kisida, B. (2017). The art of partnerships: Community resources for arts education. *Phi Delta Kappan, 98*(7), 8–14.

Bowen, D. H., & Kisida, B. (2019). Investigating the causal effects of arts education experiences: Experimental evidence from Houston's Arts Access Initiative. *Houston Education Research Consortium, 7*(3), 1–35.

Brown, A. L., Ash, D., Rutherford, M., Nakagawa, K., Gordon, A., & Campione, J. C. (1997). Distributed expertise in the classroom. In G. Salomon (Ed.), *Distributed cognitions: Psychological and educational considerations,* (pp. 188–228). Cambridge University Press.

Burn, A., & Parker, X (2003). *Analysing media texts.* Bloomsbury Academic.

Burnaford, G., Brown, S., Doherty, J., & McLaughlin, J. H. (2007). *Arts integration frameworks, research, & practice: A literature review.* Arts Education Partnership.

Ching, D., Santo, R., Hoadley, C., & Peppler, K. (2015). *On-ramps, lane changes, detours, and destinations: Building connected learning pathways in hive NYC through brokering future learning opportunities.* Hive Research Lab.

Cope, B., & Kalantzis, M. (2000). *Multiliteracies: Literacy learning and the design of social futures.* Psychology Press.

Côté, J. E., & Levine, C. G. (2002). *Identity formation, agency, and culture: A social psychological synthesis.* Lawrence Erlbaum Associates Publishers.

Darling-Hammond, L. (2007). Race, inequality and educational accountability: the irony of "no child left behind." *Race, Ethnicity, and Education, 10*(3), 245–260.

Dewey, J. (1916). *Democracy and education.* MacMillan.

Dewey, J. (1938). *Experience and education.* Macmillan.

diSessa, A. (2004). Metarepresentation: Native competence and targets for instruction. *Cognition & Instruction, 22*(3), 293–331.

Edwards, C., Gandini, L., & Forman, G, (1991). *The hundred languages of children: The Reggio Emilia approach—Advanced Reflections.* Elsevier Science.

Eisner, E. (2002). *The arts and the creation of mind.* Yale University Press.

Eisner, E. (2004). What can education learn from the arts about the practice of education? *International Journal of Education and the Arts, 5*(4).

Enyedy, N. (2005). Invented mapping: Creating cultural forms to solve collective problems. *Cognition & Instruction, 23*(4), 427–466.

Fey, T. (2011). *Bossypants.* Little, Brown and Company.

Fisher, D., & Frey, N. (2013). *Better learning through structured teaching: A framework for the gradual release of responsibility,* 2nd Ed.. ASCD.

Fleming, M., Bresler, L., & O'Toole, J. (2015). *The Routledge international handbook of the arts and education.* Routledge.

Freire, P., & Macedo, D. (1987). *Literacy: Reading the word and the world.* Bergin & Garvey.

Gay, G. (2007). The rhetoric and reality of NCLB. *Race, Ethnicity, and Education, 10*(3), 279–293.

Gee, J. P. (1989). Literacy, discourse, and linguistics: Introduction. *Journal of Education, 171*(1), 5–17.

Gee, J. P. (2007). *What video games have to teach us about learning and literacy* (2nd ed.). Palgrave Macmillan.

Glass, I. (2009, July 11). *Ira Glass on storytelling 2* [Video]. YouTube. https://www.youtube.com/watch?v=dx2cI-2FJRs.

Goldstein, T. R., & Lerner, M. D. (2018). Dramatic pretend play games uniquely improve emotional control in young children. *Developmental Science*, DOI: 10.1111/desc.12603

Gonzalez, H. B., & Kuenzi, J. J. (2012). *Science, technology, engineering, and mathematics (STEM) education: A primer.* CRS report for congress. Congressional research service 7-5700. www.crs.gov R42642.

Graue, E., Hatch, K., Rao, K., & Oen, D. (2007). The wisdom of class-size reduction. *American Educational Research Journal, 44*(3), 670–700.

Graue, M. E., Whyte, K. L., & Karabon, A. E. (2015). The power of improvisational teaching. *Teaching and Teacher Education, 48*, 13–21.

Green, J., & Kindseth. A. (2011). Art all day: distinction and interrelation of school-based and out-of-school arts learning. *Studies in Art Education, 52*(4), 337–341.

Gutstein, E. (2006). *Reading and writing the world with mathematics: Toward a pedagogy for social justice.* Routledge

Haddon, M. (2003). *The curious incident of the dog in the night-time.* Doubleday.

Halverson, E. R. (2005). InsideOut: Facilitating gay youth identity development through a performance-based youth organization. *Identity: An International Journal of Theory & Research, 5*(1), 67–90.

Halverson, E. R. (2007). Listening to the voices of queer youth: The dramaturgical process as identity exploration. In M. V. Blackburn & C. Clark (Eds.), *New directions in literacy research for teaching, learning and political action* (pp. 153–176). Peter Lang Publishing.

Halverson, E. R. (2010a). Film as identity exploration: A multimodal analysis of youth-produced films. *Teachers College Record, 112*(9), 2352–2378.

Halverson, E. R. (2010b). Detypification as identity development: The dramaturgical process and LGBTQ youth. *Journal of Adolescent Research, 25*(5), 635–668.

Halverson, E. R. (2013). Digital artmaking as a representational process. *The Journal of the Learning Sciences, 22*(1), 121–162.

Halverson, E. R. & Gibbons, D. (2010). "Key moments" as pedagogical windows into the digital video production process. *Journal of Computing in Teacher Education, 26*(2), 69–74.

Halverson, E. R., Litts, B., & Gravel, B. (2018). Forms of emergent collaboration in maker-based learning. In J. Kay & R. Luckin (Eds.), *Rethinking learning in the digital age. Making the learning sciences count* (pp. 1304–1311). International Society of the Learning Sciences.

Halverson, E. R., Lowenhaupt, R., Gibbons, D., & Bass, M. (2009). Conceptualizing Identity in youth media arts organizations: A comparative case study. *E-Learning and Digital Media, 6*(1), 23–42.

Halverson, E. R., Lowenhaupt, R. & Kalaitzidis, T. (2015). Towards a theory of distributed instruction in creative arts education. *Journal of Technology and Teacher Education, 23*(3), 357–385.

Halverson, E. R., & Peppler, K. (2018). The maker movement and learning. In F. Fischer, C. Hmelo-Silver, S. Goldman, & P. Reimann (Eds.), *The international handbook of the learning sciences* (pp. 285–294). Routledge.

Halverson E. R., & Sheridan, K. M. (2014). The maker movement in education. *Harvard Educational Review, 84*(4), 495–504.

Hardiman, M. M., & John Bull, R. M. (2019). From STEM to STEAM: How can educators meet the challenge? In A. J. Stewart, M. P. Mueller, and D. J. Tippins (Eds.), *Converting STEM into STEAM programs: Methods and examples from and for education* (pp. 1–10). Springer.

Hattie, J. A. C. (2009). *Visible learning: A synthesis of over 800 meta-analyses relating to achievement.* Routledge.

Heath, S. B. (2000). Making learning work. *After School Matters, 1*(1), 33–45.

Hetland, L., & Winner, E. (2004). Cognitive transfer from arts education to nonarts outcomes: Research evidence and policy. In E. W. Eisner & M. D. Day (Eds.), *Handbook of research and policy in art education,* (pp. 135–161). Lawrence Erlbaum.

Hetland, L., Winner, E., Veenema, S. & Sheridan, K. (2013). *Studio thinking 2: The real benefits of arts education.* Teachers College Press.

Hmelo-Silver, C. E., Duncan, R.G., & Chinn, C. A. (2007). Scaffolding and achievement in problem-based and inquiry learning: A response to Kirschner, Sweller, and Clark (2006). *Educational Psychologist, 42*(2), 99–107.

Holbert, N, Berland, M., and Kafai, Y. (2020). *Designing constructionist futures.* MIT Press.

hooks, b. (1999). *Talking back: Thinking feminist, thinking Black.* South End Press.

Hutchins, E. (1996). *Cognition in the wild.* MIT Press.

Jenkins, H., Clinton, K., Puruchotma, R., Robison, A., & Weigel, M. (2007). *Confronting the challenges of participatory culture: Media education for the 21st century.* MIT Press.

Jurow, S., & McFadden , L. C. (2005). Improvisational science discourse: Teaching science in two K–1 classrooms. *Linguistics and Education, 16*(3), 275–297. DOI: 10.1016/j.linged.2006.02.002

Kafai, Y., & Harel, I. (1991). Children's learning through consulting: When mathematical ideas, programing knowledge, instructional design, and playful discourse are intertwined. In I. Harel & S. Papert (Eds.), *Constructionism.* Ablex.

Kaufman, J. C., & Sternberg, R. J. (2010a). *Cambridge handbook of creativity.* Cambridge University Press.

Kaufman, J. C., & Sternberg, R. J. (2010b). Creativity. *Change: The Magazine of Higher Learning, 39*(4), 55–60.

King, A. (1993). From sage on the stage to guide on the side. *College Teaching, 41*(1), 30–35.

Kirschner, P. A., Sweller, J., & Clark, R. E. (2006). Why minimal guidance during instruction does not work: An analysis of the failure of constructivist, discovery, problem-based, experiential, and inquiry-based teaching. *Educational Psychologist, 41*(2), 75–86.

Knobel, M. & Lankshear, C. (2017). *Researching new literacies: Design, theory, and data in sociocultural investigation.* Peter Lang.

Kraehe, A. M., Acuff, J. B., & Travis, S. (2016). Equity, the arts, and urban education: A review. *The Urban Review, 48*(2), 220–244.

Ladson-Billings, G. (1995). Toward a theory of culturally relevant pedagogy. *American Educational Research Journal, 32*(3), 465–491.

Ladson-Billings, G., & Tate, William F., IV (1995). Toward a critical race theory of education. *Teachers College Record, 97*(1), 47–68.

Ladson-Billings, G. (2014). Culturally relevant pedagogy 2.0: The remix. *Harvard Educational Review, 84*(1), 74–84.

Ladson-Billings, G. (2017). The (r)evolution will not be standardized: Teacher education, hip hop pedagogy, and culturally relevant pedagogy 2.0. In D. Paris & S. Alim (Eds.), *Culturally sustaining pedagogies: Teaching and learning for justice in a changing world* (pp. 141–156). Teachers College Press.

Ladson-Billings, G. (2021). I'm here for the hard re-set: Post pandemic pedagogy to preserve our culture. *Equity & Excellence in Education, 54*(1). https://doi.org/10.1080/10665684.2020.1863883

Lankshear, C. & Knobel, M. (2011). *New literacies: Everyday practices and social learning*. Open University Press.

Larson, J. (2017). Critical literacies. In K. Peppler (Ed.), *The SAGE encyclopedia of out-of-school learning* (pp. 163–167). SAGE.

Lee, C. D. (1995). A culturally based cognitive apprenticeship: Teaching African American high school students skills in literary interpretation. *Reading Research, 30*(4), 608–630.

Lee, C. D. (2001). Is October Brown Chinese? A cultural modeling activity system for underachieving students. *American Educational Research Journal, 38*(1), 97–141.

Lee, C. D., Rosenfeld, E., Mendenhall, A., Rivers, A., & Tynes, B. (2004). Cultural modeling as a frame for narrative analysis. In C. Daiute & C. Lightfoot (Eds.), *Narrative analysis: Studying the development of individuals in society* (pp. 39–62). SAGE Publications.

Leep, J. (2008). *Theatrical improvisation*. Palgrave Macmillan.

Leonardo, Z. (2007). Introduction: Special issue on no child left behind. *Race, Ethnicity, and Education, 10*(3), 240–243.

Litts, B., Halverson, E., & Sheridan, K. (2020). Taking up multiliteracies in a constructionist design context. In N. Holbert, M. Berland, & Y. Kafai (Eds.), *designing constructionist futures: The art, theory, and practice of learning designs* (pp. 235–244). MIT Press.

Lobman, C. (2006). Improvisation: An analytic tool for examining teacher-child interactions in the early childhood classroom. *Early Childhood Research Quarterly, 21*(4), 455–470.

Machado, E. & Hartman, P. (2019). Translingual writing in a linguistically diverse primary classroom. *Journal of Literacy Research, 51*(4), 480–503.

Magnifico, A. (2010). Writing for whom? Cognition, motivation, and a writer's audience. *Educational Psychologist, 45*(3), 167–184.

Marino, K. (2018). *The benefits of arts education for English language learners' acquisition of the English language*. (Order No. 10752850). ProQuest Dissertations & Theses Global. (1978496358).

Markus, H., & Nurius, P. (1986). Possible selves. *American Psychologist, 41*(9), 954–969.

Marx, R. W., & Harris, C. J. (2006) No child left behind and science education: Opportunities, challenges, and risks. *Elementary School Journal, 106*(5), 467–477.

Mayer, R. (2004). Should there be a three-strikes rule against pure discovery learning? *American Psychologist, 59*(1), 14–19.

McLaughlin, M. W., Irby, M. A., & Langman, J. (1994). *Jossey-Bass social and behavioral science Series. Urban sanctuaries: Neighborhood organizations in the lives and futures of inner-city youth.* Jossey-Bass.

McLean, C. A., & Rowsell, J. (2021). *Maker literacies and maker identities in the digital age: Learning and playing through modes and media.* Routledge.

Mejias, S., Thompson, N., Sedas, R. M., Rosin, M., Soep E., Peppler, K., Roche, J., Wong, J., Hurley, M., Bell, P., & Bevan, B. (2021). The trouble with STEAM and why we use it anyway. *Science Education, 105*, 209–231. http://doi.org/10.1002/sce.21605

Mishook, J. J., & Kornhaber, M. L. (2006). Arts integration in an era of accountability. *Arts Education Policy Review, 107*(4), 3–11.

Morrell, E. (2008). *Critical literacy and urban youth: Pedagogies of access, dissent, and liberation.* Routledge.

National Academies of Sciences, Engineering, and Medicine (2018). *How people learn ii: Learners, contexts, and cultures.* The National Academies Press. https://doi.org/10.17226/24783.

New London Group (1996). A pedagogy of multiliteracies: Designing social futures. *Harvard Educational Review, 66*(1): 60–93.

Nixon, J. (2020). Merging out of school learning strategies with academic pursuits: Video production for the classroom environment (Publication No. 27963210) [Doctoral Dissertation, University of Wisconsin–Madison]. ProQuest Dissertation Publishing.

Norman, D. (1993). *Things that make us smart: Defending human attributes in the age of the machine.* Addison-Wesley Publishing Company.

Osbourn, A. (2019). Transgressing the disciplines using science as a meeting place: The science, art, and writing initiative. In A. J. Stewart, M. P. Mueller, & D. J. Tippins (Eds.), *Converting stem into steam programs: Methods and examples from and for education* (pp. 149–167). Springer.

Pace, J. (2011). Teaching literacy through social studies under no child left behind. *Journal of Social Studies Research 36*(4), 329–358.

Papert, S. (1980). *Mindstorms: Children, computers, and powerful ideas.* Harvester Press.

Papert, S., & Harel, I. (1991). Situating constructionism. In I. Harel & S. Papert (Eds.), *Constructionism.* Ablex Publishing.

Paris, D., & Alim, S. (2017). *Culturally sustaining pedagogies: Teaching and learning for justice in a changing world.* Teachers College Press.

Pea, R. D. (2004). The social and technological dimensions of scaffolding and related theoretical concepts for learning, education, and human activity. *The Journal of the Learning Sciences, 13*(3), 423–451.

Peppler, K., Keune, A., & Thompson, N. (2020). Reclaiming traditionally feminine practices and materials for STEM learning through the modern maker movement. In N. Holbert, M. Berland, & Y. Kafai (Eds.), *Designing constructionist futures: The art, theory, and practice of learning designs* (pp. 127–140). MIT Press.

Pinkard, N., Erete, S., Martin, C. K., & McKinney de Royston, M. (2017). Digital youth divas: Exploring narrative-driven curriculum to spark middle school girls' interest in computational activities. *Journal of the Learning Sciences, 26*(3), 477–516.

Project Zero. (n.d.). *Project zero's thinking routine toolbox.* Project Zero. pz. harvard.edu/thinking-routines

Pyles, D. G. (2016). Rural media literacy: Youth documentary videomaking as a rural literacy practice. *Journal of Research in Rural Education, 31*(7), 1–15.

Razzouk, R., & Shute, V. (2012). What is design thinking and why is it important? *Review of Educational Research, 82*(3), 330–348.

Richards, K., Austin, K., Gomez, K., & Gray, T. (2014). Professional development remixed: Engaging artists as teachers and mentors. In B. Barron et al. (Eds.), *The digital youth network: Cultivating digital media citizenship in urban communities* (pp. 57–96). MIT Press.

Ryoo, J. & Calabrese Barton, A. (2018). Equity in STEM-rich making: pedagogies and designs. *Equity & Excellence in Education, 51*(1), 3–6. DOI: 10.1080/10665684.2018.1436996

Salomon, G. (1997). *Distributed cognitions: Psychological and educational considerations.* Cambridge University Press.

Sawyer, R. K. (2011a). *Explaining creativity: the science of human innovation.* Oxford University Press.

Sawyer, R. K. (2011b). *Structure and improvisation in creative teaching.* Cambridge University Press.

Sawyer, R. K. (2018). Teaching and learning how to create in schools of art and design. *Journal of the Learning Sciences, 27*(1), 137–181.

Sawyer, R. K., & DeZutter, S. (2009). Distributed creativity: How collective creations emerge from collaboration. *Psychology of Aesthetics, Creativity, and the Arts, 3*(2), 81–92. https://doi.org/10.1037/a0013282

Scheurman, G. (1998). From behaviorist to constructivist teaching. *Social Education, 62*(1), 6–9.

Sefton-Green, J. (2000). From creativity to cultural production: Shared perspectives. In J. Sefton-Green & R. Sinker (Eds.), *Evaluating creativity: Making and learning by young people.* Routledge.

Smith, J. K., & Smith, L. F. (2010). Educational creativity. In J. C. Kaufman and R. J. Sternberg (Eds.), *Cambridge handbook of creativity* (pp. 250–264). Cambridge University Press.

Soep, L. (2006). Critique: Assessment and the production of learning. *Teachers College Record, 108*(4), 748–777.

Solomon, F. C., Champion, D., Wright, T., & Steele, M. (in press). Embodied physics: Utilizing dance resources for learning and engagement in STEM. *Journal of the Learning Sciences.*

Spina, S. U. (2006). Worlds together . . . words apart: An assessment of the effectiveness of arts-based curriculum for second language learners. *Journal of Latinos and Education, 5*(2), 99–122.

Squire, K. (2006). From content to context: Videogames as designed experience. *Educational Researcher, 35*(8), 26.

Steffe, L. P., & Gale, J. (1995). *Constructivism in education.* Routledge.

Stephens, S., & Haddon, M. (2012). *The curious incident of the dog in the nighttime.* Methuen Drama.

Stewart, A. J., Mueller, M. P. , & Tippins, D. J. (Eds.) (2019). *Converting STEM into*

STEAM programs: Methods and examples from and for education. Springer.

Street, B. (2017). Multiliteracies. In K. Peppler (Ed.), *The sage encyclopedia of out-of-school learning, vol 2.* (pp. 505–509). SAGE.

Triandis, H. C. (2001). Collectivism and personality. *Journal of Personality, 69*(6), 907–924.

Tseng, T. (2016). *Making make-throughs: Documentations as stories of design process.* [Unpublished doctoral dissertation]. Massachusetts Institute of Technology. http://web.mit.edu/ttseng/www/academics/papers/dissertation.pdf

Turner, E. E., Gutiérrez, M. V., Simic-Muller, K., & Díez-Palomar, J. (2009). "Everything is math in the whole world": Integrating critical and community knowledge in authentic mathematical investigations with elementary Latina/o students. *Mathematical Thinking and Learning, 11*(3), 136–157.

Tzou, C., Meixi, Suárez, E., Bell, P., LaBonte, D., Starks, E., & Bang, M. (2019). Storywork in STEM-art: Making, materiality and robotics within everyday acts of indigenous presence and resurgence. *Cognition and Instruction, 37*(3), 306–326.

United States. National Commission on Excellence in Education. (1983). *A nation at risk: the imperative for educational reform.* The National Commission on Excellence in Education

Vosniadou, S., & Brewer, W. F. (1992). Mental models of the earth: A study of conceptual change in childhood. *Cognitive Psychology, 24*(4), 535–585.

Wenger, E. (1998). *Communities of practice: Learning, meaning, and identity.* Cambridge University Press.

Whoopensocker (2020, April 10). *When I broke my arm* [Video.] YouTube. https://www.youtube.com/watch?v=ViWFG5FoRFY&t=96s

Whoopensocker (2020, April 24). *I love Harrison Ford and you can't tell me no!* [Video.] YouTube. https://www.youtube.com/watch?v=Mxfl6uTIaug

Wiggins, G., & McTighe, J. (2005). *Understanding by design.* Association for Supervision and Curriculum Development.

Wiley, L., & Feiner, D. (2001). Making a scene: Representational authority and a community-centered process of script development. In S. C. Haedicke & T. Nellahus (Eds), *Performing Democracy: International perspectives on urban community-based performance* (pp. 121–142). University of Michigan Press.

Wilkerson, M. H. & Gravel, B. (2020). Storytelling as a support for collective constructionist activity. In N. Holbert, M. Berland, & Y. Kafai (Eds.), *Designing constructionist futures: The art, theory, and practice of learning designs* (pp. 213–226). MIT Press.

Wong, C. P., & Alim, H. S. (2017). Hip-Hop. In K. Peppler (Ed.), *The SAGE encyclopedia of out-of-school learning* (pp. 117–140). SAGE Publications, Inc.

Wong, C. P., & Peña, C. (2017). Policing and performing culture: Rethinking "culture" and the role of the arts in culturally sustaining pedagogies, in D. Paris & S. Alim (Eds.), *Culturally sustaining pedagogies: Teaching and learning for justice in a changing world* (pp. 117–138) Teachers College Press.

Yahner, J., Hussemann, J., Ross, C., Gurvis, A., Paddock, E., Vasquez-Noriega, C., & Yu, L. (2015). *Strengthening youth through the arts: Evaluation of the Arts Infusion Initiative.* Chicago Community Trust.

Index

About the Author

Dr. Erica Rosenfeld Halverson is a trained theater artist and award-winning professor in the Department of Curriculum and Instruction at the University of Wisconsin–Madison. In that role, she teaches a range of courses to undergraduate and graduate students, including future teachers. Halverson has been a field leader in the learning sciences, creating a subfield that focuses on how people learn in and through the arts. Erica is a seasoned performer and cofounder of two community youth arts programs: Whoopensocker (Madison) and Playmakers Lab Theatre (Chicago). She also performs regularly, working with the Children's Theater of Madison, Four Seasons Theatre, and Music Theatre of Madison. She lives in Madison with her husband Rich and her daughter Gracie.